CW00923394

TRAINING THE SHEEP DOG

Training the Sheep Dog

Thomas Longton & Barbara Sykes

The Crowood Press

First published in 1997 by
The Crowood Press Ltd
Ramsbury, Marlborough
Wiltshire SN8 2HR

British Library Cataloguing-in-Publication Data
A catalogue record for this book is available from the British Library.

ISBN 1 86126 0318

Acknowledgements
The authors would like to thank Mrs O. Lieber, Mrs R. Davis, Dr V. Hebeler, Mrs A.
Hermes and Mr T. Robinson.

Photographs supplied by Paul Welch, M.E. Longton, Dr V. Hebeler, Odette Lieber,
Marc Henrie, Mrs D. Gerber-Mattli, Mrs A. Hermes, Donatella Muirhead, E. Sommer,
A. Bonner, David Harling, Burgess Photo Print, BBC Television and the authors.

Line-drawings by Annette Findlay.

Dedication
This book is dedicated to our children; they are the future.

Throughout this book, 'he', 'him' and 'his' have been used as neutral pronouns and
refer to both males and females, be they human or canine.

Typeface used: New Century Schoolbook.

Typeset and designed by D & N Publishing
Lambourn Woodlands, Hungerford, Berkshire.

Printed and bound in Great Britain by WBC Books Manufacturers, Mid Glamorgan

Contents

Foreword

It is in Britain that the working sheep dog has reached the height of skilled partnership with its handler, an almost telepathic communication between man and dog that seems uncanny to anyone watching a trial for the first time.

We have grown accustomed to seeing the best performances in some of the most beautiful countryside imaginable, each chosen to entertain on television. The popularity of these programmes speaks for itself.

When watching the stars, we should not forget the humbler, but indispensable, dogs which are kennelled on all hill farms. They go about their daily work with the same cheerful spirit and instinctive anxiety to please which enables the flock master to carry out his work. No mechanical aids have yet been invented which can replace a dog in the exacting tasks they do so willingly.

People not brought up to the job are now inspired to 'have a go', and this book, written by a member of one of the most distinguished trialling families, will be of invaluable help to them in developing a unique partnership.

As I have owned a working Border Collie, and have tried to learn with him, I am delighted to recommend this book to all who aspire to work a dog.

Her Grace, The Duchess of
Devonshire

Introduction

Would you like to train a sheep dog? Have you ever wondered what is involved in the training of the dogs you see working and trialling? *Training the Sheep Dog* is a comprehensive and practical guide to training a collie for agricultural work and, by adapting the finer training techniques, for the competitive world of sheep dog trialling.

If you want to train a dog yourself for working sheep or cattle, or hope to develop the natural instincts of the collie for other herding work, the practical information given in these pages will help you to understand the mind of the working dog and to develop it so the dog will be qualified to help you in your work. What is involved in the training of a sheep dog will be interesting not only to those concerned in the working aspect of the Border Collie, but to all lovers of this intelligent breed. Throughout you will be made aware that the sheep dog is more than just an ordinary dog: it is an intelligent, thinking animal, with the ability to understand and adapt to certain situations without our help.

Training the Sheep Dog is the key to understanding this unique breed of dog, and so to developing a perfect partner, workmate and companion.

CHAPTER 1

The Evolution of the Working Dog

To watch the modern-day Border Collie working in harmony with its handler is a marvellous experience. The interaction, or bond, between the man, his dog and the sheep is very special, with the dog being the fulcrum of the relationship. When the

Tom Longton competing with Bute in the International trials at Hyde Park, London in 1951. Both man and dog are oblivious to the vast number of spectators surrounding the field. Bute is coming in to shed off two sheep from the rest of the flock, totally ignoring the ones that are not required.

best handlers are working well with their dogs they can make it all look so easy, their performance showing a truly aesthetic quality in the way the dog works so smoothly: it is similar to watching Torville and Dean ice-skating their way to all those perfect scores, they were simply a joy to watch in action. However, behind any finished article there must be a sound understanding of the technical skills involved, and in this respect it is an advantage to understand how the present-day sheep dog has developed from prehistoric times.

Man's First Friend

We know that dog bones were found along with human bones in ancient prehistoric settlements, and there are cave drawings which show pictures of dogs helping man to hunt for food. It is fairly certain that these dogs were descended from wolves and jackals: the wolves were more pack orientated, whereas the jackal showed greater harmony with its parents so it may be reasonable to assume that the sheep dog probably has jackal blood in its breeding (along with many other common present-day breeds of dog). The jackal was found mainly in southern Europe, Asia, and North Africa to India. Like the fox it had an offensive odour due to the secretions made by a gland in the base of its tail, and it is interesting to observe that almost all present-day dogs will instinctively 'mark' any new territory they come across with a spot of urine.

The jackal was smaller in stature than the wolf, with less savage habits. It had a pointed muzzle like a fox, and a bushy tail about one third of its body length, and was greyish-yellow in colour which was ideal

The Asiatic Jackal, one of the well-known carnivorous mammals. Most modern breeds of dog may well be descended from this type of animal.

for camouflage. Jackals would come out from their burrows or caves at night to hunt, and would usually roam about in large packs. They fed on smaller animals, poultry and fruits, and they were particularly fond of carrion. Present-day dogs still have the habit of scavenging on any carrion they come across, and will nearly always roll on it to cover themselves in its usually disgusting smell!

There is little doubt that early man developed a bond with canine-type predators, probably initially as a result of discovering a litter of jackal pups and trying to domesticate them. They would hunt together and share their prey, the jackal being allowed to devour the entrails as a reward, and to encourage it to continue hunting with man. In the early days these animals would be used mainly to guard camps from predators such as wolves and other marauders, including man himself. Some modern-day dogs, such as the Maremma, are still used for this purpose: the pups are reared with the sheep from birth and so are regarded as part of the flock, showing a reaction to any intruders however many legs they may have.

The Evolution of the Working Dog

The evolution of the working dog from its predominantly jackal-blooded ancestor is in part recorded and in part speculation, and we have to rely quite a lot on our imaginations as to what the people, stock and villages of our ancestors looked like. If we could switch on a 'mental video recording' we would probably find these ancient relatives taking comfort from the jackals scavenging on the edge of the camp, because their barking would warn them of wolves in the vicinity. For this reason their presence probably came to be accepted and tolerated to a certain degree, their puppies may have been taken into the camp, and this possibly sealed the beginnings of that harmony achieved over the ages, of man with his dog. It is strange to reflect that, all those centuries ago, all our ancestors had in mind was to find an easier way of hunting to provide for their families, and a means to guard not only themselves but their stock, with no inkling of the legacy they were handing down to us.

Over the years dog and man became constant companions. The early shepherds used their dogs not for shepherding but as guard dogs, using them to ward off wolves and other predators; as we have said, the jackal will give warning as to the presence of wolves, and his barking may even have deterred possible attack, but it is difficult to imagine that his size and strength were a match against a determined attack by wolves. The shepherds would have been anxious to ensure the safety of their flocks, and it is believed they introduced wolf into their domestic dog, taking their better bitches to the woods when they came on heat and fastening them there in the hope of enticing the interest of a male wolf. The resulting pups were then brought up in domesticity, and developed into a larger, more powerful and more aggressive dog altogether. Some of them inherited too much of their wolf ancestry and would turn against the animals they were guarding and kill them; but on the whole they proved to be a valuable asset to the shepherd. Careful breeding and culling by the farmers and shepherds, even so long ago, provided them with a guard dog that was sufficiently powerful and aggressive to stand his ground but also capable of loyalty, traits which over the years have been carefully nurtured.

At what stage this early sheep dog was encouraged to 'work' rather than just to guard we are not certain, but it is easy to imagine the shepherds of those times running agitatedly and excitedly behind their sheep (not everything changes with evolution) and the dogs, sensing this excitement, probably running with them, and causing the stock to move more willingly. And it would not have taken much to persuade these men that with correct encouragement and a little education these dogs could be even more useful to them.

As the working sheep dog began to evolve from this guarding dog, man's breeding programme would have become more and more selective until eventually he had developed the forerunner of the sheep dog we know today. The original hunting dogs will have had little 'cast' in them, needing only to pursue and prey on one animal; but the ability to work a flock, to 'cast' had to be developed. In the eighteenth century these dogs were seen to have a special concentration, or 'eye' on the stock they were working, a trait which may have been introduced into their breeding from an early type of Setter. There is little doubt that different breeds have been introduced to the original sheep dog prototype, giving us the eye, speed, cast and stamina we need in the dogs that work for us today.

The sheep dog was – and to an extent still is – a pack animal, and man has taken it upon himself to be the leader of the pack, controlling, guiding and utilizing the pack instinct to his own benefit. Thus man has trained it to hunt without killing, and has developed a dog capable of protecting the stock it once used to prey upon:

and over the centuries the sheep dog has developed from being just a hunter to being an intelligent thinking animal, man's first and often best friend.

This was the original sheep dog, forerunner to the dogs we have today, although collies were not a well known breed of dog until the nineteenth century, when in 1860 Queen Victoria was introduced to the breed at Balmoral and subsequently began keeping them, thus increasing their popularity. Today there are five types of collie: smooth, rough, bearded, Shetland and the Border.

The Modern Border Collie

The name 'collie' derives from the Anglo-Saxon word 'Col', meaning black. A century ago the sheep in Scotland were usually dark in colour and were called 'colleys', and the dogs, also black, were known as 'colley dogs', so little adjustment was needed for their present-day name of 'collie'. The modern Border Collie evolved on the borders of

Dogs at play before a sheep dog trial in Germany. They are showing the pack instinct that their ancestors used while hunting. A word of warning is required, however. There is always a pecking order in animals, and if two are equally matched a fight may ensue; be careful that they don't hurt each other.

Pam the hunter loves to watch the movement of the farm cat. The cat knows she is safe but nevertheless does not take her eyes off the dog.

England and Scotland about three hundred years ago, and once again selective and careful breeding has served to improve the breed. The northern terrain needed strong dogs, hardy and with stamina, and the very fact that the dogs would often be working at great distance from their handlers required that they were able to work on their own initiative. Our ancestral shepherds took a great pride not only in the breeding and working of their dogs but also in comparisons, and it is easy to imagine the arguments and challenges which might have been made as to who had the better dog! Sheep dog trials were developed in the 1870s by shepherds who found them to be an ideal way of comparing their dogs' abilities under similar conditions.

Gentle persuasion. Odette Lieber's Maid calmly works young lambs, which seldom want to go in the right direction.

Official Records

The International Sheep Dog Society (ISDS) was founded in 1906 at Haddington, and keeps records which go back further than any other organization; dogs are recorded purely on ability and not on looks or beauty. In the 1950s the ISDS began a studbook which contains a record of the births of all puppies bred by the society's members. Today, all four home countries – England, Ireland, Scotland and Wales – belong to the ISDS and continue to improve the working ability of the Border Collie.

The four countries hold a National Trial annually, usually in July or August, and from these a team of fifteen comes forward from each country to go to the International Trials which are held in September. Every year a different country hosts the International Sheep Dog Trials, and up to the time of writing England, Scotland and Wales have taken it in turns – but 1997 will see the first International to be held in Ireland. The winner of the International Trials is known as the 'Supreme Champion'; the course is over half a mile

Tim Longton senior, father to Tot, was a National Champion in the 1950s. Although there has since been a dramatic revolution in all aspects of farming, the Border Collie has not changed much in the last fifty years, but still does the work it was bred for.

Champions all, Fern, Pam, Tweed and Gem relax in the garden, next to the English National Brace Trophy that they have all won.

long, and is a supreme test for both dog and man, resulting in a true champion. Without doubt it is the most prestigious event in the world to win.

At the present time it is not possible for a world championship to be held regularly because UK rabies restrictions enforce a six months' quarantine for any dog returning to the British Isles; but it is hoped that in the future it will be easier for dogs to travel to and from other countries, and this freer movement for our collies will result in a true world champion.

In Europe there has been a huge increase in interest in the Border Collie since the 1980s, and the breed standard has improved dramatically in the last ten years. In 1985 Odette Lieber, the first 'sheep dog lady of Europe' organized the first continental sheep dog trial in Switzerland. She founded the Swiss Sheep Dog

Society in 1982, and has been a great ambassador for the Border Collie, introducing the breed to many people in Europe and giving them an insight of what it is capable of. In this respect there are many and various languages for both dogs and handlers to understand, and this alone gives massive communication problems! At the first continental trials, France, Germany, Holland, Belgium and Switzerland had representatives, and many different breeds of dog were worked, such as Briards, the berger de Pyrénées, the German Shepherd and the Huntaway. There was also an interbreed class in which the dog had to work large numbers of sheep, taking them behind the handler and through various natural obstacles. Today there are ten countries represented at the continental trials, and again this just goes to show the massive increase in interest in working

Bess (ISDS No 101142) was the Supreme Champion of 1986 on the testing course at Beaumaris, Anglesey. Here she is with her proud owner and the spoils.

dogs, for many miles have to be travelled by both competitors and spectators.

In America and Canada sheep dog trials are held annually and it is clear that the interest in the Border Collie is ever-increasing. In the American finals in 1994 some of the handlers and spectators had travelled even further than the judges, Thomas Longton and Aled Owen!

During the last ten years there has been a great improvement in the handling of the Border Collie throughout the world, and this can only augur well for the future of the sheep dog.

Working Dogs throughout the World

There are many breeds of dog that make the herding of animals significantly easier, and which have been used to good effect in their own environment. Working dogs are fascinating to read about whatever their breed, and in this chapter we hope to give a brief indication as to some of the different breeds to be found round the world. Each has individual qualities, each has in the past been used, and the breeding improved, for a particular kind

The American finals of 1994 were held in Kentucky where Thomas Longton and Aled Owen judged. Here is the winner, Pat Shannahan, and his dog Hannah, along with Roger Culbreath, the trials organizer (right). The course was exactly the same as the International Trials course held in the British Isles, a supreme test of man and dog.

of work. However, we make only general comments, because each dog will vary according to a wider spectrum.

The Border Collie is rapidly becoming one of the most universal shepherding dogs, its speed and intelligence gaining it popularity throughout the world; however, each of the breeds described in this chapter – and many more not mentioned – has qualities which make it special in its own particular field. One of the Border Collie's attributes is its ability to use the power of its 'eye' to gain control over the sheep it is working. Not all working dogs share this ability, and in some cases – for very large flocks or herds, for example – it would even be a disadvantage.

All working dogs have certain characteristics, which make them particularly useful: thus, some may 'give voice', making it easier to move the large flocks found in countries such as Australia; others find it no problem to travel over and under the stock they are working in order to reach a desired position to assist movement, once again in large flocks. Some breeds of working dog remain on their feet and are constantly on the move, whereas others prefer to keep stopping and to work at a slower pace. Not all stock dogs are used for herding: some are bred specifically to intermingle with the stock, showing no aggression whatsoever, in order to protect against marauders.

The annual show and sale of cattle, horses, sheep and other animals at Regina, Saskatchewan. In 1993 Thomas Longton was invited to take a young dog over, and here is Glen with his proud new owner, Terry.

Australian Cattle Dog

This dog evolved from stock from Scotland. Blue merle collies were crossed with the dingo to produce a dog which could stand up to the rigours of working wild cattle. Later a Dalmatian cross was used, which is probably why cattle pups are born white. Next a Kelpie cross was introduced, and although it is possible that bull terrier blood was used there is little doubt that Dingo blood was, and probably still is introduced.

Australian Kelpie

A strain of prick-eared, smooth-coated working collie developed by the early settlers from stock imported from Scotland in the 1870s. It is smaller than the Border Collie, usually full of energy, and li es to work

The Siegenthaler family show their family of Border Collies in the Emmental region of Switzerland. They have sheep that are milked daily, so these dogs have become of great assistance on the steep slopes of the mountain pastures.

The Australian shepherd has a perpetual motion style of working and can take on the most obstinate of cattle.

The Kelpie at work with Swaledale ewes in the Trough of Bowland in England. Their active close-working style suits large flocks.

close to its sheep, although some do have a reasonable gather. Kelpies are strong-willed and constantly on the move, which makes them ideal for working in small paddocks or pens. They have been trained to move sheep along a race by running to the front along their backs, then coming down to race along the ground, making the sheep move forwards as they do so. They are suited to large flocks of slow-moving sheep.

Bearded Collie

The Beardie is good-tempered, medium-sized and shaggy-coated, and has been a sheep dog for most of its history. It usually prefers to remain on its feet when working, and although it doesn't have the eye of the collie it generally keeps a steady rhythm when working. Beardies do not work silently: they were used in the Highlands because they would give voice as they approached the sheep, causing them to gather and hold together while a more silent worker, such as the Border Collie would cast out and bring the flock down to the fold. There are records of Beardies being placed at sheep dog trials in the late nineteenth century, but they are not really suitable for trials because they prefer to work on their own initiative rather than forming a partnership. Although Beardies are still used in the British Isles for both work and trial they are in a minority.

Briard

A very ancient breed of shepherd dog from France: Briards tend to be large, shaggy-coated dogs suited to slow-moving sheep. They are handsome, and work in a head-up, tail-wagging style. They can gather and do most jobs on the farm, but are short of speed for the flightier type of sheep.

The Briard of Serge Richoz working sheep in Switzerland. These large dogs have a smooth style of working and prefer a slow-moving flock of sheep.

The German Shepherd dog 'working the furrow' at a competition in Germany.
His job is not to allow the sheep to cross over the furrow without instruction
from his handler, forcing the sheep to graze in the designated area.

Catalan Sheep Dog

A Spanish sheep dog originating from Catalonia; as well as being a herding dog it is also used for droving cattle. In appearance it is similar to the Old English Sheep Dog only smaller, and is probably related to the Pyrenean Mountain Dog.

Dutch Herder

A large dog which can be rough-, smooth- or long-coated. The farmers of Holland were careful to breed this dog for its ability and working bloodlines rather than for looks, with the result that it is a good all-round farm dog capable of working in an efficient manner on most kinds of stock.

German Shepherd

The working German Shepherd is generally a large, square-shaped dog that works with no 'eye' or balance. They are trained to follow their instinct which is to 'work the furrow', meaning they will patrol up and down a boundary fence all day long. Once they understand where the boundary – the 'furrow' – is, they will keep the sheep away from that area. This is useful when moving sheep past a field of corn along the road, for example, because the dog will keep the sheep away from the corn. The term 'translumanz' is used for moving sheep during the season; long distances may have to be covered to find new grazing for the sheep, so the shepherds and their dogs stay with them the whole time.

Huntaway

A New Zealand dog, a mixture of breeds with a great deal of the British Beardie blood evident. Two types have been standardized: a rough-coated dog similar to an Old English Sheep Dog × Beardie in appearance; and a smooth-coated dog, which is most common. They are best suited for larger flocks, and are very effective at pushing sheep into pens, for example, because they have a commanding influence yet never 'grip' sheep. They also 'give voice', and never waste time on the gather because sheep will flock when they hear them barking; this makes them ideal for gathering on rough terrain.

Komondor

A Hungarian sheep dog with 1,000 years of history to its credit. Used on the Puszta, it has a pure white, long woolly coat which is usually matted and serves to disguise it amongst the semi-wild sheep it herds.

Lancashire Heeler

A small, strongly-built, little terrier-type dog not unlike a corgi in appearance. Standing approximately 30cm (12in) at the shoulder, they are said to have been used originally by butchers to drive animals into the slaughter houses. In spite of their small size they show remarkable courage and determination when working cattle, and at the turn of the twentieth century were found on cattle farms throughout the north-west of England. In more recent years, however, they have ceased to be in demand on farms, but have been saved from extinction because they have proved to be devoted companions and housedogs.

The New Zealand collie has been trained to work stealthily, applying gentle pressure on the animals before moving them. These dogs are taller and longer than Border Collies.

These Maremmas have been reared with the sheep and make excellent guard dogs. There is no chance for any intruder to cause problems with the sheep.

Maremma

Still used as a sheep dog in Italy, it can also be found in the show-ring, typified by its lovely, flowing white hair. Maremmas are excellent guard dogs, staying with the sheep and keeping everything and everybody away. It is difficult to believe how kind and gentle these dogs are to sheep, actually licking them, yet how aggressive they can be to intruders.

Polish Sheep Dog

A truly versatile dog of Poland: it has been used for herding sheep, pulling dairy and bakery carts, and as a guide and guard

dog; in addition its outer hair combings are used in upholstery and its softer undercoat combings are woven for clothing.

Portuguese Cattle Dog

Found in the north of Portugal. A large dog with a short, harsh coat, used by drovers for guarding the cattle herds from wolves.

Portuguese Sheep Dog

An extremely large, independent and ferocious mountain dog which lives and works at altitudes of over 600m (2,000ft). Like the cattle dog it is used for guarding stock.

Puli

The Hungarian Puli varies in its ability and capabilities, and its ancestry can be traced back for at least 8,000 years! It is faithful and intelligent with a pronounced sense of humour, and makes an excellent housedog as well as an efficient sheep dog. Its distinctive feature is its coat which hangs in cords and serves as a natural protection from the extremes of weather on the Puszta of Hungary.

Pumi

A Hungarian cattle dog occasionally confused with the Puli, the Pumi is adaptable and friendly but can be headstrong. It is bred solely for working cattle and swine.

Pyrenean Sheep Dog

Smaller than the Pyrenean Mountain Dog; it comes from the Spanish borders and excels both as a sheep and a cattle dog.

Rough Collie (Lassie type)

A tall, handsome, intelligent dog, which can be sensitive to criticism; very popular as a show dog, but some do still have the ability to work sheep. Their style of working is head and tail up, and although they do not have the 'eye' of the Border Collie, a keen Rough Collie can be a strong dog.

Rumanian Sheep Dog

There are two sorts of Rumanian Sheep Dog: a short-tailed, light-coloured one, and a darker long-tailed type sometimes used for draught work. An independent dog bred solely for work and extremely efficient.

Shetland Sheep Dog

The 'Sheltie' resembles a Rough Collie in miniature, his sweet alert expression being characteristic of the breed. They are mainly found in the show-ring but many do still work: they can gather, and although small, they are hardy and can be quite tough with stock. They are sensitive to handle, however.

Siberian Sheep Dog

Has erect ears and curled tail; it is used for hunting and herding, but it is also popular for its hair which is used by the natives.

Ukrainian Sheep Dog

Similar, and related to the Hungarian Komondor, and commonly used as a shepherd's dog.

Throughout the world there are many working dogs, some of them well known and some only to be found in their native lands. It is easy to be so engrossed in our own type of stock and herding requirements, and the dogs that we know so well, that we forget – or maybe do not realize – that there are so many other working dogs of such great variety and capabilities. One quality which seems to shine through in most, if not all of these dogs is their intense desire to work and to guard, and their loyalty. In this chapter we have

The judges meeting before the trial starts in Germany. The judges' box is a horse trailer, which is ideal in good weather!

selected breeds from some countries where perhaps sheep dogs weren't thought to exist; these working dogs all vary not only in style and type but also in appearance and coat texture, each being well equipped physically for the climate and terrain it has been bred to work in.

Of all the breeds omitted there is one more we would like to mention: it varies in size although it is usually compact; its colour varies, as does its coat length and texture; and it has a low-set tail. It is hardy, economical, faithful, loyal, hard-working, humorous, intelligent and very willing. We have spared just one short paragraph to it here, because the rest of the book is in fact dedicated to it: the Border Collie.

CHAPTER 2

Choosing a Puppy or an Older Dog

The type of dog you purchase and at what age is an entirely personal decision, but it should not be taken lightly: for the prospective owner of a sheep dog it is of the utmost importance. After all, the dog you choose will be your friend, companion and helper for a long time, and you should consider your options very carefully at the outset. The price of a trained dog is obviously going to be higher than that of a puppy, and it will vary according to the standard of the dog; however, a high price does not always guarantee that you will have a dog which suits you. The older dog,

Lyn keeps a careful eye on her litter of six puppies as they take breakfast from her 'milk bar'. Additional help may well be needed for bitches with more puppies.

whatever its stage of training, should be one that you can handle and that is capable of performing at work how you want it to. Remember your dog will be your friend and companion for many years to come, so it is very important that you enjoy each other's company. Choosing a collie is not a matter of just going out and buying a dog: you are choosing a working partner as well as a companion, and you both need to like and to respect each other. The initial bonding is the all-important foundation for the building of a strong and successful partnership between handler and dog, an intelligent thinking relationship.

Choosing a Puppy

The advantages of choosing a puppy are simple. You are picking a dog of your own choice, and a puppy has no possible hangups: it comes to you with complete innocence of mind, and its future development is largely your responsibility. When you rear your own puppy you develop a very special relationship together, a much deeper and stronger bond. You learn how the dog thinks, moves and behaves as it grows, and your puppy also grows to know you and your personality; it understands when you are happy with it, also when you are not. It is a very special feeling when you have reared a puppy to adulthood, have been totally responsible for its training and finish up with a dog that works well for you. There is no feeling like it; it is really very satisfying indeed!

You can choose any puppy you want, but it is important to search out the type of dog that suits you. Do not be tempted to pick out the first puppy you see, but visit as many litters and look at as many dogs as possible so that you have a comparative view of what you would like in a dog. The bloodlines in a Border Collie are very important, so check the five generation pedigree of the puppy to see if you like its genetics. Most breeders will be happy to show you the mother of the litter working sheep, and if you will want your dog to work cattle it is essential that its mother is a cattle dog.

There are many questions that you can ask the breeder. For example, has the mother had any litters previously, and if so, are they working? Take the time to go and see any offspring of the bitch that you can. The sire (father) of the pup is also important, since he is supplying half of the genetic make-up – although our own theory is that the dam (mother) of the pups is much more influential, and that her genes are more likely to influence the progeny. Some bitches are just good breeders, and mother offspring to a much higher level of consistency. The Border Collie puppy you buy should be registered with the International Sheep Dog Society (ISDS). Both parents should be registered, and should have been eye-tested by a fully qualified vet from an eye-testing panel.

Have the parents had their hips X-rayed? This is something which many breeders tend to ignore, but we feel it is very important to select puppies from parents that have sound hips. Most vets can X-ray the hips, and X-rays are then sent to the British Veterinary Association in London to be scored by fully qualified vets.

Have the puppies been wormed regularly? All puppies suffer from roundworms, and they must be wormed from three weeks of age to ensure they are healthy. When you buy your puppy, give it some worming medicine as a matter of course, to ensure it is completely free from internal parasites. Even a healthy-looking puppy may be carrying a large worm burden that will affect its future growth and health.

Do you want a dog with long or short hair? Again, this is a personal decision and you must check the parents to see if they are a type of dog you like – but you must check the grandparents and the great-grandparents, because they will also influence the genetic make-up of your pup; in fact most traits that are heritable can go back several generations. This means that you can never be absolutely sure how the puppy will work when adult, although you know you are looking for a dog that has brains, and the ability to understand what you are teaching it.

Check that the puppy is correct in its mouth, with perfectly matched teeth so that the bite is even. Some dogs may be under-shot or overshot, and although this does not affect their ability to work, it will detract from their appearance and their value for breeding since these are heritable faults. Some people prefer their pup to have a black roof in its mouth: this may be an 'old wives tale', but if it makes you feel happy then so be it – your puppy has to be what you want.

Make sure you like the general appearance of the pup, that it stands well on its legs and is well grown. And if there is anything at all that you do not like, then do not buy it. There will be plenty more pups for you to choose from. Also check what sort of conditions the puppy is living in: if you like how the dogs on the farm are kept, the chances are that you will be satisfied with your pup.

Tweed – an outstanding example of the Border Collie head. Relaxed concentration shows in the eyes of the dog.

What about me? It is difficult to resist a young puppy when he shows you his big, soft eyes.

Two of a kind. Here are two fine-looking puppies taking their first taste of snow, which has fallen overnight.

It is a good idea to have the puppy checked by a vet. He will listen to its breathing and its heartbeat, and will check its general condition, making sure it is perfectly healthy.

One of the disadvantages of choosing a puppy is that it is impossible to tell how its temperament will develop as it grows into adulthood. Even one puppy that is

Mirk encounters a cat in the garden for the first time. He explores the cat's smells and movements, showing the first instincts of starting to work.

boisterous and full of beans may become quieter as it grows; and conversely, a shy puppy may become a well tempered, care-free adult dog. The one thing you can be certain about is its markings, because its coat colour is for life and will never change.

Choosing an Older Dog

If you are going for an older dog, first impressions count for a lot. Moreover, if you like the look of a dog, the chances are that it will like you. The first thing to inspect is its physical appearance, the head being the most important part. Does it have enough room between its ears for brains? The ideal head, typical of many Border Collies, has a level top and drops almost squarely to the top of the jaw. The eyes will generally indicate a dog's temperament: preferably they

Alertness is shown here in the face of Pam, twice National Brace Champion. She seldom misses any sudden movement of any sheep.

Barbara Sykes' dog Moss shows the stalking technique with his front leg raised, which his forefathers used when hunting their prey.

should be dark in colour, and look at you in a friendly and confident manner; if they protrude excessively and dart around the dog may well be too nervous – and we cannot stress too much how important it is that a dog has a good temperament. It should look proud of itself when walking around free, happy to be alive. Regarding the ears, it is up to you whether you like pricked up or half pricked ears, or one ear up and one down, it does not really matter. We personally do not like collies with ears that hang down like those of a spaniel, this sort often tends to be lazy and sluggish. We always look for a dog that is alert and eager to please.

Another important guide to a dog's character is the shape and position of the tail, which should follow the line of the backbone and curve downwards between the hind legs. A collie uses its tail for balance when changing direction quickly and it should always hang down, because a tail which hangs too high on a dog is usually a sign of weakness – although with a young dog this may only be a sign that it is showing off to its contemporaries when loose in the yard, and in this case it is not a problem. If a young dog raises its tail high when working sheep it may be a sign of weakness, but equally it may only be a signal to the handler that it is unsure of what is expected of it, or it may simply have become too excited.

The movement of the dog when it is running is important: it should flow over the ground with ease, no matter what sort of terrain it is running over. A dog that is too long in the back may be slow to change direction, but if it has a good balance and feeling for the sheep then it will be able to cope with most situations.

The Trained Dog – the Gather

When buying a trained dog, its most important ability is how it gathers (goes round) the sheep. Watch to see if it runs too wide or too straight, and the influence it has on the sheep at the end of the outrun. This first contact with the sheep is critical, and will reflect on the way the dog handles them for the rest of the time: thus first of all it must give the sheep enough room at the end of the outrun so as not to upset them unduly. In a trial situation this initial contact (or lift) is worth ten points, and it usually sets the tone for the rest of the trial. If you get off to a good start after the outrun the judge should be suitably impressed with your dog, and this could reflect in your points. However, bear in mind that a young dog, probably one year old, may come too close to the sheep at the end of the outrun, although this may well improve with time. Our aim is to have a well trained dog by the time it is three years old, and there is no rush to train any more quickly as it will only improve through its actual experience of working with sheep; there is no substitute for giving the dog as much work as it can cope with easily.

The Importance of 'Eye'

It is better if the dog slightly overruns (goes too far) on its outrun than if it stops before reaching the far side of the sheep; if a dog constantly stops short on its outrun it is a sign that it has too much 'eye'. When a dog is working or watching sheep it requires a certain amount of concentration, but this must be flexible, allowing it to deal with two things at once: immediate control of the sheep, with the ability to remain fluid in movement in order to retain this control. A natural predator uses the power of the eye in order to produce a hypnotic effect on its prey – without flexible concentration a stalemate can result.

A dog with too much 'eye' often becomes transfixed by the sheep and thus becomes restricted in its own movement. It tends to move secondary to the sheep and is more likely to spend time lying on the ground with its head low, and will be too slow to move when the stock challenges it. It may even reach the stage of not being able to move the sheep because it is concentrating too hard on watching them and not listening to the handler. This type of dog is really only useful on very flighty sheep that are constantly moving away from the dog. Different breeds of sheep react differently to dogs and it is important to have a dog that suits your own breed of sheep.

A dog with too little 'eye' is said to be plain: it generally carries its head high and is more casual about the way it works. The good thing about a plain dog is that it seldom upsets the sheep and they do not feel threatened by it. However, its level of concentration and attention to the handler may be low, and it is generally slow off the mark to react to a command; this can be particularly frustrating if a quick response is required. When pressured by the handler it may lose concentration on the sheep altogether and go off sniffing, or just wander away and wait for something nice to be said to it.

A medium level of 'eye' concentration is ideal, where the dog has enough 'eye' to hold its concentration on both the sheep and the handler.

Temperament

It is vital that your dog has a good temperament: this cannot be stressed enough. If you expect to go to a trial where there are people, it is essential that it is not shy of them when it works the sheep. Having said that, a dog may be shy of people when it is just wandering through a crowd of spectators, but completely forget them when it is working. Or it may be scared stiff of a strange human approaching, but have the power to work the most obstinate cattle.

Working Cattle

Dogs tend to work cattle in a slightly different fashion and with different enthusiasm than they work sheep. Quite often sheep and cattle graze in the same field, so it is important that your dog is not intimidated by cattle. Tweed (ISDS 140476) preferred working sheep, and flowed behind them with perfect balance and feeling. However, when asked to move cattle he seemed to feel that this was below him and worked them in a very rough manner, quite unlike his approach to sheep. Yet Lassie had an equal desire to work sheep and cattle, and with training learned to fetch dairy cows at milking time, bringing them through the sheep when given a command of 'ho-up'. Without command she would fetch sheep and leave the cattle grazing!

It is better if your dog will ignore cattle when working the sheep, and move freely between them as they graze. If the sheep realize that the dog is afraid of the cattle, and is always circling away from them, then they will rush to the side of a cow knowing that this is a safe position to be in, as the dog will be unable to move them.

Pam shows her confidence in turning this calf around to go in the other direction.
It is good to train the cattle to respect the dog when they are young calves.

This American quarter-horse worked in perfect harmony with a dog to hold difficult sheep at the stake for the American finals in 1994.

Never take a new dog to cattle that have not seen a dog before; they are bound to become upset and will trample it into the ground if they can, and the new dog will run back to the handler and both may be trampled. Definitely not to be recommended. In this situation you must have a dog with plenty of experience so that he can look after himself when the hooves start flying. Also, it is much better to educate the cattle when young, so that they respect the dog before they become too powerful. Animals have long memories, and if they are handled firmly yet steadily they will be manageable throughout their lifetime.

Nursery Trials

Another thing to remember when looking at an older dog is that it is probably working on ground that it is used to; it may have been trained on the same field for many months, and on the same sheep, and you cannot be sure if it will perform in the same way when taken from its own environment. For this reason, nursery trials are good for young dogs: they give the opportunity to take a dog into strange surroundings and work different sheep, and sheep are always surprising in the way they behave towards a dog they are seeing for the first time.

Much more finesse has to be put into the training of your dog if you want to take it and compete at nursery trials. It is always surprising to see a dog's reaction the first time it is taken away from home to run in a trial; quite often it will look as though it has never been trained at all! However, after several weeks a dog should have become accustomed to travelling to fresh fields and running on strange sheep.

CHAPTER 3

Care and Management of a Puppy

Barbara Sykes shows how to hold a young puppy, with her hands underneath in support. It is time the puppy had a look at the big, wide world.

Rearing a puppy is neither complicated nor difficult, but a certain amount of knowledge together with a good dose of common sense is needed. Rather like building a house, you must provide a good solid foundation to ensure that you can obtain the best results.

Nutrition

The correct plane of nutrition is essential to the well-being and development of the young pup, because both growth and energy levels are affected by correct and incorrect feeding. There are many varieties and types of food available, and what some people may tell you to feed to your puppy can be truly astounding. Always remember that every puppy is an individual, the puppy itself will tell you if your feeding regime is suitable: the condition of its coat and the amount of flesh on its back are both telltale signs of good or bad feeding.

Correct nutrition does not begin with the weaned pup: it starts at its conception. Thus a bitch should be given a high level of nutrition, not only to keep herself in good order but to give the best possible start to her litter. Until three weeks of age the puppies will only be taking milk from their mother, so she should be given extra, good quality food so she will have plenty of milk for them. A constant supply of clean fresh water should always be available; the lactating bitch needs plenty of fluid.

During the first few weeks of pregnancy the bitch may alter very little in appearance, but the demands made on her body by the unborn puppies will soon take their toll if she is not fed accordingly. If you are feeding a complete food it would be advisable to increase the protein intake, especially if your bitch is still working; and if you have been feeding what may be a more unbalanced diet, for example biscuits with meat and/or additives, now is the time to consider changing to something which contains all the required nutrients in balanced form. As the pregnancy advances, so you will need to monitor your dog's dietary intake; gestation is approximately nine weeks, and as the puppies grow you may find it necessary to feed your bitch two small feeds rather than one large one – but all dogs are different, so you must feed according to your own dog's requirements. There is no harm

in a pregnant bitch being given light work too: it will keep her active and therefore healthy, and it will also keep her mind alert; but take care never to work her in a situation where she will be vulnerable, such as with ewes and lambs or strong cattle. If there is little work for her to do, or if a kennel mate has taken on her responsibilities, make sure she gets plenty of exercise and fresh air. After the birth the need for careful feeding is just as important: a good bitch will give her best to her offspring, and if the nutrition she receives is insufficient, she will be the one to suffer. Remember, a constant supply of fresh water should always be available for any dog, but the lactating bitch in particular needs plenty of fluid, so check her water bowl more frequently.

At approximately ten days the puppies should have their eyes open and be moving around, gently exploring. At three weeks they can be given a little milk substitute, gradually mixing this with porridge oats, so that the demand on the bitch is not as great. They soon become more dependent on a food supplement, but their stomachs are very small at this stage and it is better to feed them little and often until they become capable of eating larger amounts. By the time they are six weeks old they should be used to more solid food, and this should vary: thus some meals should be cereal based and mixed with milk, and others should consist of chopped meat or fish. Dogs are carnivores after all and meat is essential to their diet.

If you are buying a puppy it will probably be eight weeks old and on an established diet, but leaving the 'nest' is a stressful time and can often result in feeding difficulties. Ask the breeder what your pup has been fed on, and if possible make sure you have the same food in stock, or can beg a supply from the breeder; most breeders will provide enough food for the first few feeds as a matter of course. If you are changing the puppy's diet, this is much better if it is done gradually over a few days so that the pup has time to adjust. Each feeding session should last for ten minutes; if, after that time, there is some food left, take it away and give fresh food at the next mealtime.

All puppies require a balanced diet to give them the best possible start in life. They need the right combination of protein, fat and carbohydrate, and because they have small stomachs the food needs to be more concentrated than for the adult dog; therefore it is important that the correct balance of vitamins and minerals, which are essential for healthy growth, is also provided.

It is essential to feed your puppy a balanced diet by using common sense and a little knowledge of essential requirements. For example, milk, eggs, meat and fish are all proteins for a growing puppy; and porridge, vegetables, pasta and rice are all ingredients for a healthy diet. If you are mixing your puppy's food yourself, you must make sure you vary the content of the meals, not to give variety but to ensure you are not feeding four meals a day of high protein with nothing to balance it. There are many commercially formulated puppy foods on the market that provide a balanced diet: they are simple to use, provide the necessary nutrients and ensure your youngster is used to eating well without developing the habit of becoming 'choosy'. A puppy may soon become used to having varied meals; some he will prefer to others, and if you are not careful he may start refusing to empty his dish if it does not contain his 'pick of the day'. It is possible he may prefer one particular type of

food to another, and he may 'do' better on one particular brand, but it is a matter of trial and error to find the one that suits; all dogs are different and, like humans, the same food does not agree with them all.

Try to avoid highly coloured food; it may look good to the human eye, but it may make a hyperactive puppy even more energetic. As a general guide, try to avoid food which is nearly all cereal, because the nutritional requirements may not be enough for the working collie; similarly, some of the high-energy foods which contain both high fat and protein are usually too energy-giving, making it difficult to control your dog. A good quality food designed to give your dog the essentials needed without forcing its growth or providing unnecessary 'hype' is what you need to be looking for.

Throughout the first few months of your puppy's life you will be feeding little and often, providing balanced feeds of varying substance; by the time the young dog has reached six months of age it should be adequate to feed two balanced meals a day. These can be a 'complete food'. As his first birthday approaches, one well balanced and substantial meal a day will be sufficient, and there is no reason other than age or health why an adult dog should require more than one feed a day. The complete food can be purchased by the sack, and generally keeps well; it can be fed dry, or it can be moistened with a little warm water. As always, your dog should have a plentiful supply of clean, fresh drinking water, although if you provide the food 'dry' he will need his water bowl filling more often. There are no hard and fast rules on feeding regimes. Some dogs have a very fast metabolism and may require different amounts of food. The simplest 'rule of thumb' guide is the condition of your pup: it wants to be fit not fat, so feel its back regularly to check that it is maintaining the condition that you would like.

It is possible to overfeed your puppy in the first year of life, but this is not usual. However, note that extremely fat puppies place a huge burden on their heart and their legs, and that hip dysplasia may be exacerbated when puppies are over-weight. It is therefore most important not to overfeed, nor to give food which is of too high a quality to young dogs. A pup tre-bles in size in the first few months of its life, and then doubles in size up to five months, so it is important to make sure you adjust the nutrition accordingly. A high plane of nutrition is fed in the first few months to ensure correct growth and development, but if this same level of nutrition is fed when the young dog's growth rate has slowed down, it can cause both physical and mental damage. Good, nourishing food for the adolescent does not need to be high in energy to maintain good condition, and a dog in adolescence that is proving difficult to teach may ben-efit from a lower energy food. This does not mean reduced quality – it is simply giving the correct quality food with the correct energy level for the age and situa-tion. If you are feeding a 'complete' food, make sure that you know what the pro-tein level is: this is a guide as to the energy intake for your dog.

Gentle exercise will improve your puppy's fitness, and is a good way to check its general health; however, overstretching your young dog is not to be recommended as it increases the risk of hip dysplasia. As a general guide, let the puppy be a puppy for the first year of its life – that is, enjoy playing and working without indulging in anything too strenuous.

A Health Programme: Worming

A routine health programme for your puppy is essential for growth. One of the first problems is that the young puppy is more likely to have worms, of which there are three main types:

Roundworms

Roundworms are the most common type of gut worm and pose a threat to humans as well as animals, the main species found in dogs being *Toxocara canis*. The adult roundworms are yellowish-white in colour, have pointed ends and vary in length from approximately 4 to 10 cm (1.5 to 4in). They normally live in the intestines, and pro-duce vast numbers of eggs which pass out with the faeces. These eggs are resistant to both heat and cold and may survive in the soil for many years, so it is almost impossible for dogs to avoid coming into contact with them. Both the pregnant and the lactating bitch will also require worm medicine.

Tapeworms

Tapeworms have a flat segmented body and a small head, and attach themselves to the gut wall. Fully grown tapeworms may be extremely long, but it is more usual to see segments in the faeces. Each segment contains both male and female reproductive organs; these segments fill with eggs when mature, then break off and are passed in the faeces. In order to complete their life-cycle the tapeworm eggs must pass through an intermediate host, the most common being the flea or louse. Worm re-infestation of the dog occurs when the intermediate host is eaten, therefore tapeworms are more likely to occur when your dog has a flea infestation. This is why it is important to groom your dog regularly: brushing not only keeps its coat shiny and clean, it also gives you the opportunity to check for any parasites on the skin. If your puppy or dog is always scratching itself, this is a sure sign that it has fleas, lice or mites. It is essential to keep your dog's bedding thoroughly clean, as this can be the ideal environment for external parasites; straw in particular harbours fleas and mites. Ordinary dog shampoos may not be good enough for all types of parasite, so it may be a good idea to ask your vet what he/she recommends as best to use.

Hookworms

Hookworms are very small, approximately 1cm (⅜in) long, and as their name implies, are bent into a hook shape. Heavy infestation can lead to anaemia, resulting from the bloodsucking habit of these worms. Most hookworm infestations are usually mild, but if they are present they will need a higher dose of treatment than is required for roundworms. Not all worm treatments are effective against hookworms, so check before you buy; it is well worth the extra care.

It is wise to assume that your puppy has a worm burden at all times, so that you never forget to give worming medicines. A good worming regime is once every two weeks until four moths old, once every month until six months old, and then twice a year throughout its life.

There is a risk – though admittedly very small – that certain worms can be transmitted to humans, so please ensure regular worming, taking care to administer correct dosage for the weight of your dog.

Diseases and Vaccination

In the first few months of life a puppy is usually protected from disease by the antibodies it receives in its mother's milk. However, this form of immunity soon wears off and your puppy is then primarily at risk from four dangerous diseases: distemper, hepatitis, leptospirosis and parvovirus.

Distemper (Also Known as Hard-pad)

A virus that can affect dogs of all ages, but is most common in puppies. The first clinical sign is respiratory: the dog will have runny eyes and nose, a moist cough and sometimes diarrhoea; it will also have a high temperature and will lose its appetite. The second indication is nervous: there will be muscle spasms and twitches leading to fits and possible paralysis. The footpads and nose skin often harden (hence the name). The virus is transmitted from an infected dog in droplets of moisture and dogs usually become contaminated by sniffing where other dogs have been. It is advisable to forbid your unvaccinated, unprotected puppy any contact with animals other than your own, until the course of injections by your vet has provided full protection.

Hepatitis

A very contagious viral disease that in its acute form can prove fatal within 24 hours. It attacks the liver, and symptoms include acute abdominal pain, vomiting, diarrhoea, fever and loss of appetite. In mild cases the eyes, kidneys and respiratory organs are affected, as well as the liver.

Tot Longton with his dog Spot at a trial. Spot was one of the top dogs of his day, but was struck down with distemper when only four years old. This was before preventative vaccines were developed. It is folly not to make sure that your puppy or dog has had all the DHLP injections from the vet.

Leptospirosis

A disease caused by bacteria that is spread in the urine of infected animals. There are two major forms: one causes acute illness and jaundice and is often caught from rat's urine or a rat bite; this can also affect humans and is very serious. The other occurs more frequently and is chronic, leading to slow destruction of the kidneys.

Parvovirus ('Parvo')

'Parvo' is perhaps the most serious and most common infectious canine disease. Relatively new, being recognized only in the late 1970s, there was an epidemic of parvo in which hundreds of dogs died before an effective vaccine was produced. It is very difficult to treat, the symptoms being extreme depression, high temperature, vomiting and abdominal pain. A bloody diarrhoea soon leads to rapid dehydration, collapse and death, all in the space of 24 hours. This disease is extremely infectious and can often wipe out an entire litter of puppies, and the only protection against it is by vaccination every year.

All the above diseases are so life-threatening that it is essential that all puppies receive protection by vaccination of DHLP vaccine from your vet. This is quite simple and involves two small injections under the skin, the first when the puppy is approximately ten weeks old, and the second one within the following four weeks, depending on the pup's age and the vaccine used. If you live in a high-risk area then the vaccination may be given earlier (but please check with your vet). Make sure you receive a vaccination certificate signed by your vet, recording the date the vaccinations were given and the future annual booster dates. Please don't take risks with any of these diseases: make sure that all four are covered by the vaccine given by your vet, and remember that protection may not be fully effective until several weeks after the first injection.

Eye Diseases

There are two main inherited eye diseases that may affect Border Collies, and it is important to make sure that your puppy comes from eye-tested parentage.

Progressive Retinal Atrophy (PRA)

As its name suggests, PRA is progressive and leads to blindness; it is a disease that is due to a defect within the outermost layer of the retina. This defect leads to degeneration of those cells in the retina which transform light into nerve impulses. As it is the central portion of the retina that is involved, affected dogs will retain some peripheral vision. The disease is often not seen until the dog is five or six years old, although it may be present when it is as young as 18 months; it is therefore important that breeding stock is checked annually. Any dog failing its eye test should not be used for breeding.

Collie Eye Anomaly (CEA)

CEA can be present in a puppy at birth, therefore the ideal time for testing is when the eye is big enough to examine, between six and ten weeks of age. Small lesions in a young puppy may be masked by the growth of the eye as it ages, so it is quite possible that a puppy showing CEA at eight weeks of age may have a 'pass' diagnosis when it is an adult dog. This would not mean that the dog was no longer affected by CEA, simply that it was no longer detectable; similarly there is no absolute guarantee that an adult dog having its first examination and receiving a 'pass' diagnosis is not affected. On the other hand, a puppy that receives a 'pass' at seven weeks of age will not show CEA later. Litter screening (examining the entire litter together) provides the necessary information to ensure that only dogs that have 'sound' eyes are used for breeding; and it is worthy of mention that dogs which are only slightly affected can produce progeny that is severely affected.

The International Sheep Dog Society, based at Chesham House, Bedford, keeps a studbook of all registered Border Collies, and this includes a list of dogs that have failed the eye test. In the past decade the percentage of dogs failing the eye test each year has decreased, and out of the hundreds tested in the last twelve months the failure rate was approximately 1 per cent. This has been made possible by the vigilance of the ISDS, the eye-testing scheme and the breeders. There is no point in spending many years training a dog only to find that it has eye problems which could have been detected earlier.

Canine Hip Dysplasia (CHD)

In the British Isles, checking the hips of Border Collies is not yet regarded as a priority as it is in other countries; however, to

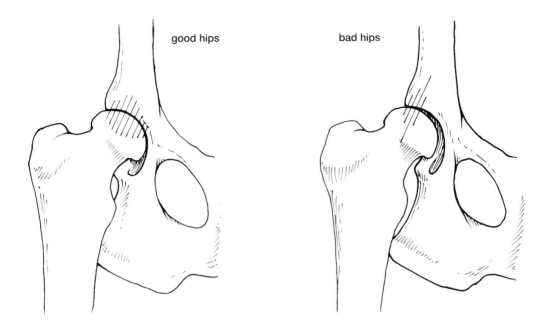

good hips   bad hips

Fig 1 Hips. The force is distributed over a small area so there is much greater stress on the joint.

ensure healthy progeny, all breeding stock should be checked.

Hip dysplasia causes stress and strain in the hip joint, and unacceptably high stress leads to the premature erosion and loss of the articular cartilage. The hallmark of CHD is a shortened stride length due to the reluctance to extend the hip, and clinical signs include lameness, joint abnormalities and the reluctance to exercise. Large and giant breeds of dog are more at risk from the disease. As well as being hereditary, there are other factors which influence the level of hip dysplasia. The rate of growth, feeding methods, food consumption, specific nutrients and electrolyte balances may affect the condition or cause hip damage. Known nutritional risk factors are rapid weight gain and excessive calcium supplementation.

Dogs with well conditioned muscles and good strength tend to compensate clinically for CHD better than those with weak muscle support.

Overfeeding for maximum growth rate has been shown to be incompatible with optimal skeletal characteristics in rats, pigs, cattle, horses and also children. It has been shown that rapid weight gain in German Shepherds during the first 60 days after birth was associated with CHD at a later stage. From studies it has been felt that the first eight months of life in the dog are the most critical in affecting CHD in later life.

There is absolutely no point in pumping puppies full of energy-rich foods, vitamins and minerals. People tend to overfeed because they want their pup to grow big and powerful, but this belief is completely

A travelling box for your dog should be large enough for him to stand up in with room above his head and enough space to turn around easily.

misconceived and adult size is not determined by how much food the animal has consumed in the first year; although lack of correct nutrition may stunt growth, overfeeding can cause obesity, deformity and severe lameness.

To sum up, CHD is a complex issue that can be made worse by overfeeding the young dog; there is also an inherited risk, but this is controllable by selective breeding.

A Puppy's Social Needs

Equally important to looking after your puppy medically and nutritionally is looking after its mental welfare, and establishing that fundamental relationship you need to make a working team. The most significant time for introducing a puppy to external social influences is in the first few months of its life, and what it learns

Pam has the ability to pop her head through the vent in the sheep trailer. She has always been a nosy parker!

in this period will affect it forever; thus any action or noise that instils fear into it when it is young can cause it to react nervously when it is older. It is important therefore to remain calm and reassuring if anything startles it, for example.

Until a puppy has been vaccinated you must be careful where you take it, but try to introduce it to different sounds and surroundings; for instance, it is a good idea to familiarize it with travelling in the car as soon as possible. Also at this early stage you will be able to determine its developing character and to ascertain whether it is of introvert or extrovert nature, and this will guide you as to how you should handle it. The extrovert puppy will be interested in anything and everything, always exploring and inquisitive; the introvert will be quieter, slightly more nervous and more dependent on you for reassurance – it needs to be given the confidence it is lacking, and often responds better to quiet, gentle handling. The extrovert puppy is usually full of confidence but could get bumptious, and will need gentle, firm treatment to help him understand that you are the leader. It is important to appreciate that even in these early months, whatever the temperament of the puppy, correct handling right from the outset should obtain the desired end result: a working partner.

Its Practical Needs

You need to consider very carefully where and how you are going to keep your puppy. Although five-star is not necessary, a clean, dry warm and draught-proof bed is essential. Free exercise is important to its growth development, and the puppy should accompany you as often as possible, but it will not benefit from being left to wander round all day on its own. It is therefore good policy to provide a pen or run for the youngster to spend some time in when you are busy; as long as shelter, fresh air and clean water are provided, it does no harm for a young dog to have some 'thinking time'. However, make sure when you provide this pen, that although there should be plenty going on to keep the puppy interested, he will not be sitting watching other dogs working and fretting himself into a nervous state. There is no particular design or format that you must

Young Charlie cannot understand why the sheep is upside down, so he comes closer for a smell. All that is happening is that the sheep's feet are being checked.

The two pups, Meg and Ty, have plenty of room to play in, as well as a dry shed to sleep in.

follow when deciding on your dog's accommodation, just as there is no rule which says your puppy may or may not spend the first few months of its life in the house. It is not difficult to adapt a building or stable to make satisfactory housing for a dog, and a wire door will allow in plenty of light and fresh air as well as enabling him to see out. Furthermore, there is no shortage of choice of ready-made kennels and dog runs if you wish to purchase one, or to copy if you are handy at DIY! Whatever

The wooden dog kennel provides a warm little haven from the snow and ice of winter. Spot takes a peep before venturing out.

the size of kennel or building you use, make sure that there is a small draught-proof area for your dog to use as a bed. Most dogs feel more secure in a small 'den'; also when the weather is cold, they radiate their own heat, and they will be far warmer in a small sleeping area. There is plenty of choice when selecting bedding, shredded paper, blankets, hay and straw to mention just a few, but remember that hay and straw will harbour fleas and mites, so keep checking for these. All bedding needs to be thoroughly cleaned and aired regularly.

If your dog's sleeping accommodation does not provide visual access to the outside world you must see that during daylight hours he is either with you or has a separate exercise run or yard. A dog with nothing to do soon becomes bored and will turn to bad habits such as chewing or tail biting. To realize your dog's full potential his mind must be kept alert and active. It should also become part of your daily routine to make sure that his pen is clean, that any soiled bedding is removed, and that there is a plentiful supply of fresh drinking water. One last word on accommodation: if the weather is hot and you are not taking your dog with you, make sure that his run provides him with shade from the glare of the sun. Make sure your puppy is introduced to walking on a lead; apart from the fact that he will not always be able to run free, he must also understand some discipline. If you venture on the trial field at a later date your dog must be under control and will probably have to be fastened up, so it will do no harm for your young dog to learn to be fastened or chained up for a short time. However, on no account should a dog be left on a chain for hours on end; and when you are teaching your dog to be fastened up, always keep an eye on it, and make sure it

You can take a horse to water but you cannot make him drink, and the same applies to your dog. As long as he has the chance...

cannot jump over anything while on the chain, otherwise it could hang itself.

Remember, these are the formative months, so make sure your puppy understands what you are teaching it, and don't be frightened to spend some time playing with it; this is all part of the learning process for both of you. This is the time you are laying the foundation for that special relationship with your very own thinking dog.

CHAPTER 4

Learning to Understand your Dog

Training is a learning process not just for the trainee but for the trainer, too. Just as you need to teach your dog all the commands and requirements for working sheep, you have to learn to understand what he is thinking and feeling. A sheep dog is not, and never will be, a robot, so trying to train him to respond to your every whim without a thought for what he is, what he needs, and perhaps more importantly, what

Barbara Sykes with her dogs Pip (left) and Skye.

he is trying to communicate to you, is training for yourself and not for a partnership. So a wise dog handler will make sure he understands his dog, and will try to communicate with it whenever possible.

There is no set time when you need to say 'Today I will try to understand my dog', because like children, understanding begins in the cradle. Watch your young pup closely and you will begin to pick up messages he is transmitting. To begin with they are simple: you will know when he is hungry or thirsty because he will indicate by going to his dish or to the nearest trough or stream; you automatically know what he is saying to you by his body language and the look in his eyes, just as he knows when you are going to put a lead on him or are going to take him to the sheep field – like you, he reads messages your body and actions are sending out. So having established that you and your dog are capable of communicating on this very basic but necessary level, all you have to do is increase your levels of awareness and start to 'think' dog!

'The longest journey starts with the first step.' It is also fair to say that unless you enjoy your puppy and it enjoys you, you will never have that special relationship that you should desire. From the moment you choose your puppy it ceases to be a dream and becomes a reality; it is no longer an 'it' but a living being which is dependent on you for many things, one of the most important being guidance. It is essential to develop a rapport with him as he grows; thus, talking to him whilst he is feeding, and playing with him enables him to become accustomed to you and to learn his name. The more you encourage him and communicate with him, the sooner he will realize that when you call you are talking to him.

Introducing your Dog to the Human Language

It is important to remember throughout all training that the young dog has a virgin mind: in other words it knows nothing of the human language except what humans choose to teach it. And, if those responsible for teaching are inconsistent or muddled, this is bound to confuse the dog, making it difficult for him to understand you, and therefore difficult for him to do your bidding. Watch a fully trained dog working sheep and you may see the handler almost having a conversation with it: through their experience of learning, training and working together, the actual commands have become almost telepathic, and this conversation is their way of communicating. This type of relationship is built on creating a partnership where each is trying to help the other. A good dog trained and handled correctly will try and help its handler as much as possible when working, and a good handler will try and make it easy for the dog to give that help.

It is not difficult to understand your dog and to be able to anticipate what he is going to do, and once you have learnt to 'read' him you are on the way to having a successful and happy partnership. To begin with, however, you need to think carefully when you are introducing your dog to the human language. For example, it is a mistake to repeat commands: so, if you ask him to lie down and, after waiting for a response that doesn't materialize, you repeat the command, this is as good as telling him the command to lie down has to be repeated before it need be obeyed. Show your dog what you want: thus if you want him to lie down at the first time of asking, then make sure that he does so by pushing him to the

Gem (left) and Tweed take a break from moving the sheep into a new field. They are at the peak of their career and have full understanding of what is required when working.

faithful and everything that the individual handler dreams his dog will be; but to achieve any of the final attributes takes time, patience and hard work, and perhaps above all respect, because without respect there is no foundation for the other qualities to be built on. Respect and loyalty should be part of the puppy's education and automatically a part of his development. For instance, when you let your youngster out of his pen, don't just let him tear off into the wide blue yonder without a thought for you. After all, he wouldn't have any freedom if you had not opened the door of the pen: this freedom was granted by your discretion, not simply by the opening of the door, so make sure that before he rushes off to enjoy it, he sits for a moment and enjoys your company first. It sounds simple and matter of fact, but it is very easy for a busy person just to open the door every morning and let the dog go – and then he or she wonders why it isn't so responsive at a later date. A few extra minutes spared in the beginning can save hours of frustration later.

ground with your hands. And don't complicate matters by throwing sentences at a dog that has not yet mastered single words: 'Lie down there and stay, I'll be back in a minute, so don't move' is a waste of words and will only confuse. Keep your commands short and simple, and remember that your dog will only learn what you teach him; thus there is little point in commanding him to do something if he has no idea what you are talking about.

Teaching Respect and Loyalty

The ideal dog when trained is not only a good working dog, he is also loyal and

Building up an Understanding

The more time you can spend with your puppy, the sooner you will understand each other. For instance, if he is not accustomed to his name you will find it difficult to call him back when he is some distance away from you. All youngsters will, at some time, endeavour to 'play the fool' and try to get their own way – they may not come back when called, or they may take off in the other direction and concentrate on playing with whatever crosses their path. Inevitably this is the start of bad habits. There is no point in chastising your puppy when he does come back, because this will make him even more reluctant to come back to you and so only exacerbate the problem; therefore always talk kindly to him, stroke him liberally – however furious you might feel! In this way he may realize that he is not going to be scolded or kennelled when he is caught. It is at this stage that your early communication will pay dividends: keep a constant contact with your puppy, both physical and verbal, and he will always look to you for guidance, nor will he ever stay too far away from you for any length of time because you will have become one of the most important things in his life.

If your pup is to be looking to you for direction, encouragement and company, this in itself should tell you that it is not a good idea to allow him to spend all his time in the company of another dog. Company of his own kind is good, but not to the point where he seeks that company in preference to yours. Thus two pups growing up together will often become dependent on each other to the exclusion of the handler, so it really is essential that they spend some time apart. A pup spending all his time in the company of, and running with an older dog may learn from it, but unless you can claim to have a 'perfect older dog' – and we have yet to meet one! – he will also learn a few tricks and bad habits from it, as well as becoming independent of his handler.

So from the very early stages you can lay the foundation for respect, simply by thinking carefully before you teach and by looking at the world and yourself through your dog's eyes. Don't be frightened to play with your pup; after all, a bitch will spend hours playing with her litter – this is how she teaches them, because she also commands all the loyalty and respect possible

from them, and gets it! A pup doesn't need to play to the point of hysteria: it needs to have fun and learn in the process, though be careful not to encourage too much using of teeth, for what is harmless in a young pup may not make you happy when he practises on sheep!

Easy Discipline

Don't be too hard on your pup when he steps out of line. There is a difference between being mischievous and playful to being downright disobedient, and all pups will make mistakes – mistakes are part of the learning process. And allow your youngster the freedom for a little mischief: like children, they have to find their own boundaries and learn the ones you impose – although also like children, they must be conscious of you and realize when enough is enough. A firm 'No' when your pup oversteps the mark is not enough if he doesn't understand what the word means, and he will never understand if you don't make him stop whatever it is he is doing when you are teaching the word. 'Explained' correctly and used in the right context, the word 'No' should be a key word for your dog, automatically bringing his attention to you and causing him to question what is wrong if he does not already know.

Adjusting to your Dog

All dogs are individuals so you will probably have to adapt and adjust to suit both yourself and your dog. Some dogs have voracious appetites and some eat very little; some dogs like plenty of bedding and others will constantly rake all your efforts out of the kennel door. Some dogs respond to very quiet handling and a soft voice, appearing nervous if the handler shows stress, and others will 'feed' from the handler's stress and become over-excited. Once you understand your dog's disposition you are on your way to anticipating how it will react to different situations.

Prevention is Better than Cure

Learn to 'read' your dog's body language, because you will always have a warning of what he intends to do, even if it is only a split second. In the course of your basic training, watch your dog carefully: thus, if you tell him to lie down, keep a close eye on his body because if he decides he is going to move away from you, before he

actually commits himself to movement he will give you an indication either by leaning to one side, or twitching a muscle, or turning his head. Each dog will have its own body language and an experienced handler will 'read' his dog's intentions automatically, but the novice handler has to learn this communication. To go back to our example, once the dog has moved from the 'lie down' position to pursue his own interests, he has succeeded in doing as he wishes, and repeating the command is in fact now a separate command. If, however, you are watching and 'reading' your dog, you will be able to ensure that he remains where he is by anticipating his intentions.

If all this sounds complicated, go back to simple basics in your mind: thus you can

The television crew from How Do They Do That? *All Lad wants to do is continue working with the sheep.*

'read' when your dog is happy, sad, hungry or thirsty, and perhaps also when he is going to jump up, bark, not recall or play; you know all this by his body language, and what you must do now is 'extend' this to other exercises and 'read' a little more quickly so that you are anticipating.

Always make sure that you are near enough to your young dog to ensure that he carries out your wishes; for instance, if he doesn't come back to you in the farmyard, there is little point expecting him to come back from the sheep field! And rest assured, the first time your dog sees sheep, you are not going to be the first thing on his mind anyway – so if you have poor command of him when there is little around to rouse his instincts, you are not going to get his attention at all when he is 'having fun' with the sheep! Moreover, if a dog escapes into the sheep field without permission so that its first introduction to stock is running wildly about, using its teeth and chasing them, it may then take some convincing that this is not the way things should be. Prevention is definitely better than cure.

Remember you are dealing with an intelligent animal which is capable of learning quickly, sometimes so quickly that if you are not careful you may inadvertently teach him the wrong thing. Many a conscientious novice handler, anxious not to let the youngster loose with the sheep too soon but trying hard to build a relationship with it by keeping it with him as much as possible, has entered a large field with the dog on a lead trying to cast (outrun) round them, but in fact it is forced to walk straight up the field by its well meaning handler. The dog's natural instinct is thus curbed; it will probably still follow its instinct when it is allowed loose, but if it is a dog with little natural cast it

is virtually being told by its handler that it has no need to go round the field edge.

Here is another situation which can be prevented: if your sheep are close to the yard and you have a keen pup you may find it is constantly sneaking off to the field to 'work'. However, there is little point in admonishing it for this when soon you will be wanting it to show interest. Make sure you keep an eye on your pup, therefore, and call it to you before it manages to escape into the field; if your initial training of always making sure you are important to your dog has been done well, you will find it easy to recall him.

If you learn to study your dog's language not only will you find it easier to understand him, but you will also be able to anticipate his movements in the sheep field when you start your initial training: when you give him a command to go round the sheep you will be able to tell by the look on his face or by the twitch of his muscles whether he is going to go the way you ask or not. Once again, prevention will be better than cure, because if you can judge where he intends to go you will be able to prevent him from taking the wrong action to your command. This is one of the reasons that we advise the use of the round training pen, because it is easy for a novice handler to misread the direction the sheep intend to take and therefore give a command to the young dog which goes against its natural instinct. In the round pen you can dictate the pace of things more easily and can allow yourself time to judge the movement of dog to sheep and therefore give the correct command for the level of training you are at. Just as there is no need to rush your dog's training, nor do you have to learn in a given time. Only move forward to the next stage when both you and your dog are ready.

The True Partnership

Learning to understand your dog can help you to compensate for the shortcomings in its abilities. For example, a dog showing too much 'eye' (staring at sheep and refusing to move unless they do) can often be made to respond to the handler's encouragement, if this is given at the right time. You will also be able to judge if your dog needs help, confidence, holding back or shooing on, by his reaction to each different situation. Learn to know and understand your dog and the messages it is trying to convey to you, and you are well on the way to forming the bond needed for a perfect partnership.

Teaching your Puppy to be 'Way-Wise'

Before you take your puppy to sheep it is paramount that you have already developed a mutual understanding that he will come back to you when called, also that he shows a sensible attitude to the environment around him. He must also learn about the different sights and sounds that exist around his home – for example, the noise from the tractor or motorbike may be terrifying to a young dog. The motorbike or 'quad' is used on many farms nowadays, and your pup will find it much easier to accept if he can see you sitting on

Fern is jumping into the dog cage in the back of the car. It is good to take your dogs for a ride, but they may suffer from travel sickness just like we do. It is much safer to have a cage, as the boot lid may open whilst in transit with disastrous consequences.

Cattle are naturally inquisitive and have come to see what Pam is doing in the next field.

it; however, familiarizing him with the tractor is not as easy, because you will disappear from his sight when you are sitting in the cab. Give him the chance to become accustomed to the sight and sound of the tractor whilst he is with you, perhaps let him ride with you on occasion so he is quite used to the fast movement of modern machinery. Take him in the car with you as often as possible, because he will need to be a confident traveller if you decide to enter sheep dog trials; and if he is unhappy or frightened in the back, tie him gently in the front passenger 'well' so that you can stroke him and talk encouragingly to him to build up his confidence.

As you take your puppy around with you he will develop a wider outlook on life. This can only be to the good as what we are trying to develop is a wholly tolerant attitude from the puppy towards everything he comes into contact with. Whatever his temperament he will benefit from being taken around with you: a dog that is 'full of beans' and constantly chasing about will teach himself to settle as he tires; a shy dog will come into contact with many things that may frighten him, and a reassuring word or stroke from you will help him to gain in confidence. Learning to assess the nature of your puppy is bound to be to your mutual advantage in his future training.

Within reason it is best if your pup can learn by his own experience: for instance, if he gets too close to the wheel of an empty barrow, let him find out for himself that it is not a comfortable experience if it runs over his foot. This will help him realize that heavier things such as tractors and cars should be treated with the utmost respect.

Like a child, a puppy will draw its reaction from you. Thus if you panic in a difficult situation, then your pup will probably do likewise: it is much better to talk to him calmly, whether it be in reassurance or as discipline; remember that praising him will always strengthen the bond between you. If you start a training session with the intention of finding fault ('I'm going to put that right today!') then the session will become a chore for you both. Yes, faults have to be cured, but not to the exclusion of everything else.

If he does something you do not like, say 'No' in a stern voice. The tone of your voice is very important and your puppy will soon learn when you are pleased with him and when not. Always keep your lessons short at this stage, as the concentration span is like that of a child – very short. And if training is not going well, then stop and leave it until the next day; give both yourself and your puppy time to reflect on what has happened – say, overnight – and the following day it may go much better.

Collar and Lead Training

When your puppy is about ten weeks old it is time to fit him with a small collar. This needs to be tight enough so that he cannot slip his head out, yet loose enough for him

A simple training kit consists of: (1) a chain lead with a swivel clip – chain is best because the puppy cannot chew through it; (2) a wide collar that spreads the pull of the chain over a larger area and so is less likely to hurt your pup; (3) a whistle, plastic or metal, depending on what you prefer, or you may be able to use your fingers; (4) a crook – no shepherd looks the part without a crook, usually made from hazel and sheep's horn.

*Tying your puppy to an immovable object teaches him to be patient. After all,
it may not always be possible to have him loose with you all day. These periods
of rest are good for the dog to think over what has happened earlier in the day.*

to breathe easily; also a wide collar is preferable as this will not cause him any discomfort if he struggles to resist it. Allow him a few days to get used to his collar before introducing him to a lead; then rather than having to pull him along on a lead with him resisting you at every step, try fastening him to a kennel or some immovable object. It is best to use a light chain for this, because he will soon develop the art of chewing through a leather lead or string, and this habit will remain with him for the rest of his life. On more than one occasion will some handler have been seen to tie his dog up, and within five paces of walking away it will be right there beside

him with the remains of its chewed lead dangling from its collar! Obviously your puppy will not like being restrained and will resist the chain, perhaps furiously; nevertheless, talk soothingly to him and stand back a little to observe. Unless he is throwing himself around uncontrollably, leave him for a few minutes; then go back and give him plenty of praise before releasing him to run around at will. It is important that your puppy does not blame you for his being tied up, otherwise he will become difficult to catch at rest times. The next day leave him tied a little longer, until he is perfectly happy and contented to be left alone without being able to see you. It is good to teach him that he cannot be with you all the time, and he must learn inner patience and contentment whilst he is alone.

Now your puppy can be taken on the lead (or a light chain lead) for a walk. No doubt he will dig his heels in and resist, but talk to him calmly and in a matter-of-fact voice, some such thing as, 'Good dog, come on, let's go,' and walk for about 10m (30ft) at normal walking speed, so that he has little time to resist the forward movement. After 10m (30ft), stop and praise him with a gentle word and touch. By repeating the exercise a few times he will become familiar with what to expect, and will stop resisting when you set off for a short walk; and after a few days he should be completely happy with the lead.

It is a bad fault for a puppy or young dog to be continually pulling in front of its handler; this habit quite spoils the enjoyment of going for a walk, making it into a tiresome chore. It is much better if your puppy walks alongside and slightly behind you: in this position not only can he see in front, he can also see your movements without having to turn his head. If he constantly pulls forwards make the lead quite short and hold it behind your back instead of by your side so that he cannot circle in front of you. If he does manage to get in front, give him a gentle nudge with your legs as the lead tightens, and he will quickly realize that it is much safer to walk alongside rather than in front. Keep your dog flexible; never condition it to walk to one side only.

Lead training is essential if you are going to take your puppy to different places. Note how Barbara has her hands held behind her back so that the pup is not able to get in front of her and trip her up.

We do not recommend the use of obedience leads (choke chains); if the puppy is left alone for no matter how short a time, as long as it takes to put the kettle on, he may choke himself if he catches it on anything. It is far better to give him a firm tug on a wide collar to show him he is doing wrong.

Charlie is having his first introduction to a long, light line. He is not sure how long it is, but he realizes that he cannot chase after the sheep like he would wish to.

Once your puppy is used to being tied and walking on a lead, you can teach him to come back to you. using the 'That'll do' command. Tie a 5m (16ft) length of light cord (three pieces of bale string will suffice) to his collar, and leave him loose for five minutes. When he becomes used to it, take hold of the end and call his name, followed by 'That'll do'; should he try running in the opposite direction you have hold of him, and you can gently pull him back to you giving him plenty of praise for coming. Repeat this several times, and at varying distances so that he never knows how long the cord is.

Teaching the Lie down

Once your puppy is competent at walking on a lead you can begin to teach him to lie down – but let us stress here that the 'Lie down' command must be a happy command. This cannot be emphasized too much, for many people use this command when their puppy has done something wrong, and so comes to associate it with a punishment. So, take your puppy on a lead and gently push him to the ground, saying 'lie down' at the same time. Give him lots of praise for doing this, and then let him get up, walk with him a few yards and then ask him to lie down again. Repetition of this will teach him the 'happy' lie down. If your pup is uninterested leave him alone; do not keep forcing him to do it.

We introduce the whistle command for the puppy to lie down at the same time. 'Writing' a whistle command is practically impossible, but here goes: 'Lie down! – 'weeeu'; this is a long piercing sound and is more or less universal to all sheep dogs.

When your puppy knows to lie down while next to you, it is time to teach him

Gentle pressure from the fingers should be enough to make your pup lie down. Here Barbara shows the correct technique for calming the pup as she lies him down.

to stay down as you walk backwards a few steps. Keep him on the cord so you have more control, and if he gets up (which he will do) go back to him showing him the palm of your hand, and ask him to lie down again. You may have to repeat the command as you walk backwards. At first go only a couple of steps, and if he stays down then call him to you with 'That'll do' (and his name) and give him lots of praise. Remember, 'Lie down' must be a happy command. Our aim is to say the command and then walk away 20m (65ft) or so without the puppy moving before he is called.

If your puppy understands about lying down and coming back to you when asked to do so, you will have a much better chance of him being manageable when you take him to the sheep.

Summary

- All this time that you are spending with your puppy you are becoming accustomed to his ways, and he is learning the same about you. Thus, he will soon learn to what extent you will be tolerant of his misdemeanours before your voice changes to a sterner sound.
- You must be aiming to have an instant reaction from him, so that he concentrates on *you* and is happy and quick to respond to your voice.

- Teaching your puppy basic obedience will be invaluable later when he is introduced to sheep, because when he first sees sheep he will no doubt forget everything he has previously learnt. It is a special and unique experience for a pup when suddenly he has the urge to work sheep, and his concentration can be so blinkered that he will not hear anything you say – until, of course, you jog his memory.
- The basic obedience of your puppy will be the cornerstone of all future training, and we cannot emphasize enough the importance of spending a happy and constructive time with him. It is a learning time for both of you, and you should both enjoy it.

Introducing the Puppy to Sheep

As your puppy grows you will be watching its behaviour, how it plays and how it responds to everything in its environments, and no doubt you will be building up a picture in your mind as to how it may react when it is first introduced to sheep. The temptation to introduce it to sheep just to see what its reaction will be is often irresistible, although we always make sure that an older dog is available to make sure that the sheep do not disappear into the 'wide blue yonder'. Otherwise make sure that you create a 'safe situation', so that your sheep cannot run away and your puppy cannot be outrun.

The pup's first sight of the sheep moving. It is most interesting to see how a puppy will react to the sheep movement. At this stage all we would like is for there to be a little interest, as the sheep are much faster runners than the pup. When the puppy grows and matures he will soon be fast enough to be given more freedom.

'What's that sheep hiding in there for?'
It is impossible to expect a young dog to
bring out a sheep in this situation; you
can see that he is looking for advice.

just watch your puppy for a few minutes, and note his reaction to the sheep. Is he wanting to chase, is his head and tail down in a 'thinking position', is he bold or nervous? He should not be given any 'new' commands at this stage, as this will only confuse him; just issue the 'recall' after he has had a few minutes with the sheep, so as to bring him back to you.

If your puppy shows little interest at this age, there is no cause for alarm; he will have noticed the sheep, and may give them extra thought when you put him in his pen for the night. At some time his natural instinct will be aroused – it may be at the sight of a cat, or ducks, or even hens – not all pups develop at the same age or at the same speed. His body language will reveal his attitude to sheep, and if he is ready to think of his contact with sheep as work rather than play; you will be looking for him to drop his head a little, and his body to take up more of a hunting or stalking position with his tail down between his back legs. Something very special happens in a dog's brain when he starts working, and this is what makes a working dog exceptional.

When a puppy is introduced to the sheep with an older dog he is often more interested in chasing and trying to play around with the dog than he is in sheep. But eventually he will transfer his interest to the movement of the sheep, you will recognize this change in his attitude because he will drop his head, indicating that instinctive desire to control is taking precedence over playfulness. At this stage you need ask no more of your pup: his reaction to the sheep and his body language will tell you of his desire to work sheep. This is not a training session, it is an introduction and should only be treated as such; therefore do no more than

The Influence of 'Eye'

A dog can become so focused on whatever it is working that it ignores everything else going on around it. It may ignore everything that you are saying, even though it was well mannered when no other animals were present. We have already talked about a dog's 'eye', or its concentration when working: maybe now this will be more relevant.

A young dog with too much 'eye' will allow his attention to become so transfixed by the sheep that his body will all but freeze: this will usually be most apparent

Barbara's young Hope is poised to spring into action. All she has to do is say the command and he'll be off round the sheep.

when the sheep are facing him. He will lie with his body and head flat to the ground and become a 'stalker', only moving when the sheep move; furthermore he will find it difficult to take commands from you because of his intense concentration. Dogs like this are best suited to very free-moving sheep, ones that are constantly trying to run away. 'Heavy' sheep – those which just stand until they are forced to move – are of little use to the dog with too much 'eye' because a stalemate situation tends to arise, and even if you manage temporarily to break his concentration, he will quickly 'lock' back to the sheep, making both training and working difficult. Training with flighty sheep, on the other hand, means

that you will be able to command movement in your dog, so that he learns to move to your instructions, and can shake off the strong concentration that causes him to 'eye on'.

At the other extreme, a pup with too little 'eye' – a 'plain' dog – does not lower his head at all, and generally prefers to work on his feet; also his movement may be slower than it should be, as he tends to be more casual about his work. However, this sort of dog will not upset the sheep because they do not feel as much threatened as they would be when faced with the dog with too much 'eye', who encroaches on their 'fight and flight' distance; and so instead of facing the 'plain' dog, they will tend always to keep moving. It is important to remember that because the 'plain' dog tends to be a little sluggish and his concentration level is low, it is best to work him for a short time only. Try to build his desire to work by encouraging him to go faster, and then as soon as his mind wanders (or preferably before), stop training and try again another day.

First Steps in Training

The tone of voice and sounds that you make are the first noises of encouragement or discouragement that your puppy will hear, so it is important that you know his temperament and adjust your voice accordingly. As a general rule, 'shushing' sounds are for encouragement because they tend to excite a pup and increase its desire to move forwards. If your pup is extremely keen to work and constantly on the move, however, these sounds will seldom be used, and he is more likely to hear strong, clear commands; his brain will be easily excited, and will therefore need calming sounds. The very keen youngster can be so focused on the sheep that he will only hear you if you shout in his ear! Now is the time to put a light line onto his collar so that you can give him a tug to obtain his attention without having to shout unduly: your dog has to learn to listen to you.

Walking the sheep around the pen with young Kate still on the outside, so that the sheep will realize that there is no escape. The next task will be to ask Kate to go around the pen until she is directly opposite the handler.

Kate is being walked around the inside of the pen still being held by the line. She is pulling forward in a desire to work the sheep.

Eyeball to eyeball. Kate has moved too close to the sheep, so that the sheep dare not take her eyes off the dog and so will not turn round. Kate must now be taken by the string that is still tied to her to allow the sheep to move away.

Until you actually take your pup into the field and allow him contact with sheep, you have no way of knowing what his reaction will be. You need to be looking for signs that he wants to hold the sheep together by moving sideways , and it is truly fantastic if a young dog casts far round to the far side of the sheep and holds them to his handler straightaway, – but this is seldom the case. Very often he will not cast wide, but instead runs towards the sheep, precipitating a chase; in this instance the sheep will usually run towards a fence where the young dog may then try to 'hold' them. You know then that you can progress in your training a step forwards by encouraging him to hold them to you.

Whatever the initial reaction when you first take your dog to the sheep, as long as he wants to work then you will be able to train him to be a good working sheep dog. Remember there is no rush to train him, because his attitude will change as he grows; he will develop his own style of working and will interact with you and your teaching, and it is to be hoped that you will finish with a good friend and helper.

Using a Crook

There is no substitute for patience and forethought. We do not recommend a crook in the early stages of training; a stick-shy dog

Exuberant young Charlie has been giving the sheep too much pressure so one of them has decided to make a quick exit. Charlie cannot understand what has gone wrong; he thought he was having fun, but the sheep thought otherwise.

can be a problem, whether you are working or trialling, and at some stage you will need to use a crook in both. A young dog, particularly if he is excited at his first introduction to sheep, can sometimes misread the presence of the crook, especially if the handler is showing excitement or stress. Let your dog become accustomed to seeing you with a crook while around the farm or out walking, and you can introduce it into your training when he is more confident and you are working together in harmony.

The Round Training Pen

When you introduce your young dog to sheep for the first time you may find it all too easy for both sheep and dog to get out of control, and the round training pen is a way of creating a situation that helps you to keep control. If you choose to try your dog without the aid of the pen you will probably find that your sheep, on sight of the dog, will make a dash for the nearest corner. The keen youngster will enjoy asserting his new found 'power' and will endeavour to hold the small flock at his mercy, while you find yourself in a predicament trying to push the sheep back into the field against your dog. The round training pen provides a smaller training area, and ensures that the sheep remain obtainable for the young dog. The pen consists of a circle made from a 50m (164ft) roll of sheep netting with twenty-

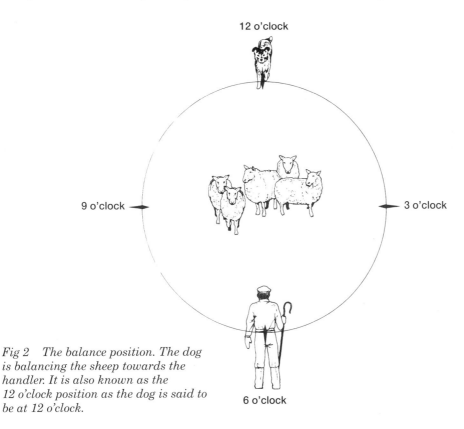

12 o'clock

9 o'clock

3 o'clock

6 o'clock

Fig 2   The balance position. The dog is balancing the sheep towards the handler. It is also known as the 12 o'clock position as the dog is said to be at 12 o'clock.

Kate, still on the outside of the pen with string attached, watches as the sheep are moved inside the pen. It is up to the handler to stay opposite the sheep until Kate realizes she can do the job herself.

taken into the pen, so you have to tailor your training to suit the needs of your own dog. Some may become aggressive if they feel they are too restricted, others may 'freeze' and refuse to move easily.

It is best to site your pen in a corner so that it does not encroach into the field too much. It should be about 3m (10ft) from any fence or wall boundary so that there is enough room for the young dog to go round with confidence. If you do not have an older dog to help you put your sheep in the pen, a little corn can work wonders, and having your pen in the corner of the field will enable you to make a funnel to run your sheep into the pen gateway. It is a good idea to walk the sheep around inside the pen so that they realize there is no escape. This is best done without a dog being present, otherwise they may bolt straight into the fence and possibly knock it down! Sheep in a confined space need to become accustomed to the 'new' dog and to feel they are in a safe area.

The first time the dog is allowed into the pen with the sheep is very exciting for both the dog and the handler, and it helps to have a more controllable situation than you would otherwise have if the sheep were free in the field. We believe the round training pen is beneficial for most dogs in the initial stages – although there are some dogs for which it may not work. However, as long as you are careful and do not expect too much too soon, there should be no problems with this method of training.

It is important to keep the sheep quiet, and not let them be frightened by a boisterous young dog, which will probably scare them straight through the fence. The round training pen is a most valuable training aid, where quality training can be given to the youngster with much less stress on both dog and handler alike.

five posts, giving a diameter of approximately 16m (53ft).

The size of the pen may need to vary according to each individual dog and its needs. Preliminary training with the dog outside the pen will benefit from the above-mentioned size; anything larger and the dog may lose 'contact' with the sheep. When you take the dog inside the pen it may be advantageous to increase the size slightly, because a young dog may feel pressured in a small pen. Each individual dog will react differently when

Kate is still held on the line and is being walked around the outside of the sheep in the pen. When the sheep move towards the centre she will be released so that it is easier for her to circle the sheep.

Lad always has a friendly stroke both before and after being inside the round training pen.

If this is the first sheep dog you have trained, and you have not kept sheep before, then you need to know a little about what is required.

Basic Practical Requirements
Initially you need a small field – an ideal maximum is 2 acres (0.8ha) – with a round training pen (*see* page 65). Should your puppy's first inclination be to chase the sheep, the limited space in this training paddock not only makes it easier for you to catch it but also spares your sheep unnecessary stress. The position and construction of your pen is important.

Breeds and Types of Sheep
Although the breed of sheep you choose to keep is up to you, that choice may be somewhat governed by the part of the country you live in. Basically the breeds are divided into two categories: hill sheep and lowland sheep. Hill sheep are usually found the further north you travel; they are smaller and hardier than the heavier lowland sheep, and are therefore more nimble of foot. The hardier sheep will adapt to the lower land, but you will not find the heavier lowland sheep on the hills because they cannot tolerate the climate. Lowland sheep are more prolific and breed a heavier lamb better suited for meat production. Although some breeds of sheep are more common than others, and you will probably make your choice from one of the main breeds, at the time of writing there are thirty-four main British breeds, twelve minor breeds, eight rare breeds, eight different strains of half-bred sheep, three southern hemisphere breeds and eight recent introductions, making seventy-three in all!

The sheep you choose for your training need to be free-moving and should not show any aggressive tendencies towards your puppy. The normal requirement is usually about six well grown lambs or hogs; Herdwick hogs (one of the main British breeds) are an ideal choice as they are generally small and easily handled. However, any breed may suffice provided they match the requirements of being calm, free-moving and non-aggressive.

Maintaining a Healthy Flock
Good management of your sheep is vital not only for their welfare but also for your training requirements, because sheep which are not in the best of health will not be able to cope with being worked regularly by a dog. You will gradually fall into a routine regarding the care and health of your flock, just as you have with your puppy. One of the first priorities should be a regular worming regime, and if the sheep are not already vaccinated, inject them to protect them against clostridial diseases. Be warned that sheep are very nimble and can often 'turn the tables', so try not to join the list of shepherds who have accidentally caught their finger in the needle point whilst trying to hold the patient still. No harm done, but both pride and finger will suffer for a while! Once on a vaccination programme your sheep should only need 'boosting' once a year, according to the vaccination instructions; however, they will need regular dosing for worms throughout the summer months to keep them healthy. If the grass is very fresh they may scour (produce loose stools), and the back-end fleece will need to be trimmed/shorn to keep it dry and clean: if they are allowed to remain dirty they could develop a fly problem and you will either have to dip them or treat them with a systemic 'pour-on-the-back' medicine.

The wool grows rapidly during the warm summer months and your sheep will need shearing. Usually contractors are engaged to clip large numbers of sheep, and they use electric shearing machines. However, if you have only a small number of sheep and are feeling

A sudden heavy fall of snow means that the sheep cannot find any grazing and so have to be given an extra feed of hay to keep them alive.

energetic they could be clipped with hand shears. This is a dying art, you will struggle to learn it, and your first sheep will probably take you all afternoon – but you will speed up with practice!! Arrangements can usually be made with a local shepherd to have your sheep clipped with his in return for help on the day.

During the winter there is a higher risk of the sheep suffering from fluke, which affects the liver, so regular dosing is required. Some breeds of sheep suffer from lameness, or foot rot, and this will be more prominent during the wet months; however, it can be alleviated by trimming the hooves with a knife or with foot trimmers and spraying with an appropriate antibiotic or foot-rot spray.

Caring for the sheep and maintaining them in a healthy condition will help them stay fit and ready for training your dog. They will also improve in condition so when you part with them they will be more valuable.

Never keep more sheep than you can cope with easily, primarily so there will be grass available for most of the year. If you have too many, additional feeding may be required, and sheep used to being fed on a regular basis are not good to train a young dog on – as soon as you go into the field and the sheep see you, they will come running to your feet looking for feed and will not move away from you. Not only can this be very alarming for the young dog, not to mention its handler, it makes it very difficult for the youngster to learn to drive the sheep away, since they dart back to your feet at every opportunity almost knocking you down to get to the 'grub'.

Sheep everywhere – the pens are full to overflowing. The sheep in the field have to be left there while the ones in the pens are sorted.

The sheep are hungry after the heavy snowfall. They lose all fear of humans when hungry so the dog is used to keep them from trampling over Jenny while she is feeding them.

Sheep will eat whatever you throw at them and will always want more, so try to maintain their fitness without them being too fat. Overweight sheep tire very easily and become difficult to move, and during the heat of the summer they will become stressed. On the other hand, sheep which are too thin will not be able to cope with the pressure the young dog will put on them, and will stand and turn on it if they are harassed. Often they will lie down on the grass and 'play dead'. This totally confuses a young dog, and the result is that it will have to be called off the offending sheep while it recovers. While it is doing so it would be a wise move to gather the remainder of the flock and unite them with the single, for trying to take one sheep anywhere on its own is the most difficult of operations and should only be undertaken by the more experienced dogs.

Sheep Suitable for Training
In the early stages of training it is best to have 'heavy' sheep which like to cling to your feet; then the young pup will never be too far away and will quickly learn to go round the sheep instead of chasing them away. Flighty sheep are not good for training; they run away as soon as they see the dog, and this encourages a youngster to chase after them instead of going round the outside. The training pen must be used for this type of sheep, provided they will go in and stay in! Nervous sheep must be given time to settle in the pen without the dog, and should be walked round to learn there is no way out. Some sheep can soon learn to jump over or through the wire pen, and once they start to do this it becomes impossible to keep them inside; so it is vital to be careful when the sheep are first placed inside the training pen.

At lambing time everyone has to lend a hand. This little boy is feeding a lamb, whose poorly mother is not yet able to feed her herself.

Steady sheep make it easier for your pup to listen to you. If everything is chasing, then the puppy is so focused on the sheep he becomes blinkered and cannot hear your commands. He will learn to stop more easily, and be much easier to control, if in the early stages of this training the sheep are quiet. At a later date, when you have control of your dog, it can be beneficial to change your steady sheep for some a little more wilful in order to test him.

The progress of early training should never be rushed; it can take months just to teach the pup to hold the sheep to you, and is probably the most difficult part to achieve. It is worthwhile thinking about where and how you are going to start, and prepare a few sheep especially for the job. It can be so frustrating to go into a field and chase the sheep round for ten minutes, and teach your puppy only bad habits. It is much wiser to organize your training so that it is easy for both you and your puppy to enjoy a quality time training together.

Pushing back the Horizons

As your puppy matures and his training progresses, you must start to vary the field of training and also the sheep, so that the dog has its mind stretched! Bigger outruns can help to steady a very keen youngster, and giving a dog more freedom may result in him trusting you more. If you go back to the same old routine of training month after month, then your dog will become bored and 'stale'.

If you want to go to a sheep dog trial, your dog must be well adjusted to different people, different sheep and different fields, so training at home must give it the same challenges. These challenges and different situations help to build up trust and to develop the partnership between you and your dog.

Not all sheep are to be found in a flat field. Here the sheep are in a dangerous position with a steep bank behind them. The Border Collie shows his skill by waiting for the sheep to drift away from danger: any sudden movement from the dog may prove fatal to a nervous sheep.

CHAPTER 5

Early Training Using the Round Pen

After teaching basic obedience and establishing a partnership, the next step is to teach your young dog to bring the sheep towards you, and to this end what we call the 'clock theory' can now be used.

The Clock Theory and 'Balance'

Imagine that you have before you a large clock: you stand at, say, six o'clock with the sheep at the centre of the 'clock face', and the idea is to have the dog at twelve o'clock, directly opposite you, and therefore 'balancing' the sheep between the two of you. This will establish the foundation of the working partnership.

To begin your training you need your sheep inside the pen and both you and your dog on the outside. Attach a light line, approximately 5m (16ft) long, to your dog's collar, then let him go and watch his reaction. If he is interested in working he will probably run straight towards the sheep, but then the pen should stop him and direct him around the outside edge of the 'clock'. Young dogs are bound to react differently: thus, some will run round and round the pen in one direction until they are exhausted, whilst others may crouch down at the first sight of the sheep and not move.

Once the youngster has expended his initial burst of energy you must try to assess his reaction to the sheep and the pen. As we have said, your aim is to encourage him to be at the opposite side of the sheep to you, so that when you move round the perimeter he moves so as to remain opposite you – although remember the partnership, in that as the dog moves, then you must move too, trying to keep the sheep in a position between yourself and the dog. At this stage we do not try to stop the dog by using the 'lie down' command, which he already knows. All we want is for the youngster to enjoy working round the pen, keeping the sheep 'balanced' between himself and the handler.

The Enthusiastic Worker

If the dog is chasing wilfully round the pen trying to get in and wanting to 'grip' the sheep, then you must be firmer and insist on a stop or a 'lie-down'. You may find it an advantage to take him away from the sheep for five minutes in order to get his attention and reinforce the 'lie-down' command. When a youngster is very enthusiastic his mind becomes totally focused on the sheep and how quickly he can get to them, so you have to

Lad has arrived at 12 o'clock, or the balance position, on the sheep. Once he realizes that this is the basis of all future training he will be introduced to the basic commands.

give louder and clearer commands to obtain his attention. Sometimes a young dog will chase round the pen in the same direction uncontrollably; in this case try to stop him with the 'lie-down' command, then send him in the other direction to obtain the 'balance' position. And if he contrives to run round and behind you, even though you are trying to block his path, then stand yourself at the side of the pen that is close to the boundary fence, and in this way you can more easily prevent him from running past you and madly chasing round. After a while he should have learned about maintaining the balance point, so that he runs back to it every time he passes it.

What you don't want is for a youngster to be running backwards and forwards continually, so use your voice to steady him down. You will need to alter your tone of voice to get his attention, and when you do break through his concentration he should slow down because he will not be sure what you are asking of him; and as he does so you can tell him to 'Take time'. Eventually even the most enthusiastic young dog will realize there is little point in chasing endlessly round, and after a few lessons will settle down to 'balance' the sheep. Always keep the lessons short at this stage; after all, a young dog has only a short concentration span, just like a child – although having said that, you may find that the more enthusiastic youngster can be worked for longer periods, because it may need to run for a while to release the tension in its body before it will settle to work sensibly.

The tone of your voice, not what you actually say, is the signal to the dog to slow down or speed up. At this stage you are not trying to teach the youngster precise commands: all you want is for him to go round the open to the far side of the sheep and 'balance' them sensibly between himself and you, so that no matter where you move, the dog will compensate by moving back to a position opposite you with the sheep in between.

The Careful Worker

There are several reasons why a youngster may be careful in its approach to sheep. Quite often its desire to work is not fully aroused, in which case all it may need is a little extra time to mature; time away from sheep and a relaxing of pressure can often work wonders in stimulating natural instincts. There is no way anyone can teach a young dog that has no desire to work, and if you persist or pressurize it, the result can be the reverse of what you are striving for: a young dog under pressure can lose the will to work altogether, and will try to leave

Kep shows his natural balance in turning this truculent sheep towards the pen. The dog's reaction is many times faster than the handler's, and if he can work on his own instinct, the sheep will soon realize that there is only one way to go.

Tip shows superb balance as he holds the sheep towards the fence. Notice the sheep are held stationary but do not feel threatened by the dog.

This technique of quick movements and stimulating noises can also be used for youngsters with a lot of 'eye' who are crouching and whose attention is wholly transfixed by the sheep. This sort will not usually move as long as the stock remains still, and in this situation you will have to get inside the pen to make the sheep move in order to get some movement and response from the dog.

The careful worker will often learn to balance the sheep in a shorter time than the more enthusiastic one; nor will he upset them with sudden movements. However, the fact that he is easier to train will not necessarily make him the better dog in the long term, so do not lose either heart or patience with the enthusiastic dog because he will settle down eventually.

Dog, Sheep and Handler in the Pen

This is a most exciting time for both dog and handler, and those crucial first few moments provide a very special 'buzz'. To start with, take hold of the 3m (10ft) length of rope attached to your youngster's collar, and hold him with a normal lead length. Give him a couple of 'lie-down' commands to settle him, and then, to allow the sheep a chance to become accustomed to the idea of the dog being closer to them, walk round inside the pen holding him close to you. After a few circles, lie him down and make him stay, hopefully giving you time to walk round the sheep yourself so as to 'balance' them between you and him. Unfortunately this is not always possible, because the action may start early!

Your efforts now are to try to keep the sheep between you and your dog, and to try and minimize the risk of your dog becoming

you when you approach the sheep, usually going to the gate to wait for the earliest opportunity to dodge back to the kennel!

If your dog is careful, shy or nervous, you will need to give him plenty of encouragement. Sounds beginning with 's', such as 'shoo' or 'shush' will generally encourage a dog to move. The speed of your movement will also affect the way he reacts: thus moving quickly and making 'shooing' sounds can excite him and stimulate his instincts, although you must be careful not to move directly towards him or behave in a manner which could make him feel threatened.

too excited, do as much of the running and 'balancing' as you can yourself to begin with; then hopefully your dog will remember to steady himself when you raise your voice and tell him to 'Take time'. Anything can happen the first time you allow your youngster free access to the sheep, but you should make a conscious effort not to stop him every time he runs too close to them – and remember, he will only stop willingly when he has the sheep between you and himself, when he is at the 'twelve o'clock position'. Your aim is still to keep the sheep between you and your dog, so that when you move sideways he too will move so as to restore the relative position of himself to the sheep. By keeping at opposite sides of the clock you 'balance' the sheep between you.

The Enthusiastic Young Dog

The enthusiastic youngster will be very direct towards the sheep and may go straight at them as in position 1 in Fig 4. If he does, step forwards at the same time to block his direct line to the sheep, therefore encouraging him to go round them towards position 2. You must be careful not to stop the youngster in his tracks: you are trying to divert him round the outside, and if you step forwards too far as he is running, he may suddenly change direction and go on the other flank. Nevertheless, although this is not what you wanted, it has to be acceptable, for at this stage the objective is to teach the youngster to go round the sheep and establish some feel for them, and to

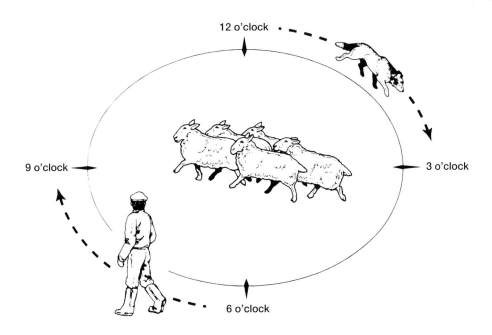

Fig 3   As the dog moves in the early stages, the handler makes a mirror-like movement so that the balance position is maintained.

Before shedding can begin, the sheep have to be balanced between man and dog. Here Alan Jones shows how to split the Welsh sheep.

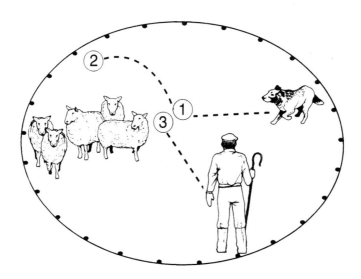

Fig 4   Young dogs may want to go straight for the sheep. As the dog moves to position 1 the handler moves to position 3, encouraging the dog to go around the sheep in the direction of 2.

Where are those sheep? Kep scans the horizon as he starts the gather on the moorland, trying to spot any movement of the sheep. Kep's posture is balanced and relaxed even though he is concentrating hard.

achieve this you cannot put too much pressure on him. No particular commands will be given yet, just gruff-sounding noises if he gets too close to the sheep, and increasing in volume the closer he gets. Keeping the enthusiastic worker at a distance will help to prevent your sheep becoming upset.

The really enthusiastic youngster may even split the sheep by diving through them. Use the 'lie down' command to try to restore some equilibrium, and before you allow him to move again, take hold of the line on his collar. Now walk round the sheep slowly to allow them to settle before you let him go again, and this time if he is too lively use the line to insist he listens to you when you say 'lie down'.

The Careful Youngster

The careful worker will be much easier on the sheep as he will move around slowly, stopping on his own without command. In fact you may find he does not want to move at all because he is so transfixed by the sheep, only moving when they do. A great deal of encouragement is therefore needed, by moving the sheep yourself and giving 'shushing' sounds to try to free the dog of his inhibitions.

At this stage it is important to avoid any confrontation between dog and sheep, so the handler must keep an eye on the sheep, and help to turn them if they look as if they might challenge the youngster.

Teaching the Dog to Leave the Sheep

A young dog finds it difficult to leave sheep when they are moving around, and it is then better policy to move away from both sheep and dog (Fig 5), at the same time calling the dog's name and saying 'That'll do'. This action of retreat will help to draw the young dog away from the sheep, and bending over will also draw the dog towards you – if you move straight towards him in an upright posture he will find this threatening, and such an attitude will usually have the opposite and adverse effect of moving him away from you. In this situation, if you hold on to the end of the line before calling him back to you, then you have a 'safety net' if he fails to come at the first time of asking.

You may also have a problem with your dog not wanting to leave the sheep when you have finished, so again, make sure you keep hold of the line which will still be attached to his collar, before you call him. Stand to the side of the sheep – no dog will want to leave sheep if he is in the 'balance' position – then bend over, pat your leg and call his name; if at this point he decides to run behind the sheep, you can give a little tug on the line, and he will soon realize that coming to you is all he can do. Always praise him for coming back to you no matter what problems he has caused you before, because it is impossible to train a dog that does not come back to you happily; if he thinks he is going to be punished, then he will probably stay out of arm's reach, and may even develop the bad habit of looking for other sheep to work.

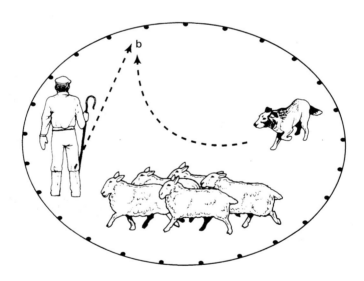

Fig 5 'That'll do' (calling the dog back to the handler). If the handler moves away from both sheep and dog (b) whilst calling his name and 'that'll do', the dog is encouraged to leave the sheep without any pressure.

The Value of the Tone of Voice

We stress that you must not be using the 'lie down' command in a gruff voice, especially if things are going completely wrong. In the early stages always say 'Lie down' when the dog is in the twelve o'clock position, for that is when the command is most acceptable to him. If he is causing problems, shout 'Hey!' or 'No!' to get his attention. It is also of more benefit if you use the dog's name regularly so that he becomes accustomed to it; varying the tone of how you say his name will enable your dog to relate how happy or annoyed you are with his behaviour. In fact it is possible to train a dog completely by using its name only, because the differing tones of the human voice can be detected by a dog's extremely sensitive hearing. However, we are not going to be so brave! In the next chapter we will discuss the commands which are simple and traditional to use whilst training your dog.

First Tenets of Training

Teaching your dog to 'feel' the sheep and find the 'balance' point is all you will have achieved by now. It may sound simple, but

At the end of the Supreme Sheep Dog Trial five collared sheep have to be separated from fifteen others and then taken to the pen. Here the dog balances the five collared sheep towards the pen, completely ignoring the others, which have been allowed to go.

Balancing the sheep on the drive. The sheep seldom want to go in the right direction, and so the dog has to find the right position from which to direct the sheep.

basically this is the cornerstone of training and will be the driving principle of the whole of the working dog's life. If you become isolated from your dog and completely out of his hearing, then you should be able to rest in the confidence that, as a result of your training, he will eventually go round the sheep and bring them back to you in a civilized fashion. All the rest of his training is just the polishing of this major principle, of bringing the sheep back to the fold.

This early training is crucial to the future relationship between man, dog and sheep. If it is not going well, then stop and take a few steps backwards, think of a new movement or sound and try again. Keep the lessons short so that the youngster's concentration is never lost. It is very easy to put too much pressure on a young dog inside the training pen, so don't expect too much too quickly. If things are not going

well with the dog inside the pen with the sheep, then take him to the outside of the pen and refresh his memory of everything he has achieved so far.

Remember, our sole aim at the start is for the young dog to go round the sheep and stay 'balanced' behind them as you move round the pen. If your young dog will do this, then it is possible to do small tasks around the farm. To us this is a crucial time in the dog's life, and it can greatly reduce future problems if the youngster develops a feel for the balanced position right from the outset.

Summary

- Training lessons should be kept short, no more than ten minutes, so that you and your dog stay fresh and alert.

Raymond MacPherson keeps his dog, Chips, on the perfect balance point as he pens the sheep after his winning run at the Deerplay Hill trials of 1996.

No escape. The sheep are being watched by Pam and Kep (left) after they have given one of their displays at a show.

- In the early stages a dog's memory, like a child's, is very short and so your instructions have to be at the right time: five seconds later and the dog will not understand what you are complaining about!
- Throughout all the crucial initial training you should be trying to assess your dog's capabilities and how to proceed with your training tactics as you introduce commands. You are not just training your dog, you are trying to build a foundation for a trusting partnership, and to do this you must be in contact with your dog's reactions and thoughts.

sheep, and you have allowed this instinct to help him understand their movement and their reaction to this dog's method of work. He has been allowed to dictate his own direction, with the handler merely following to adjust his own movement. Now that you, the handler, have the trust of your dog inside the pen with the sheep, the youngster is starting to think for himself. You will have seen him change from a juvenile (probably delinquent) towards being a thinking dog, and you can now gradually begin to introduce some more commands to increase your control.

Introducing Commands

So far the young dog has been encouraged simply to use his instinct when with

Directional Commands

At this stage in training, until you find your commands are automatic, it is a good

Kep is being shown where the balance position is in pushing the sheep and lambs through the gateway on their way back to the farm.

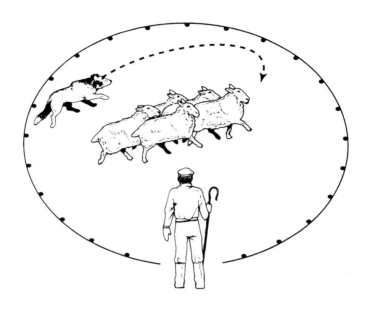

Fig 6   'Come by' is the clockwise movement of the dog around the sheep.

idea to imagine that you are with the dog so that when you give the command it is correct for the direction you want it to go. If you get it wrong, then you will have to get the next one hundred commands correct before the dog will forget the one you did incorrectly!

Due to your previous training, when your dog is working sheep he will want to return to the balance at twelve o'clock. If the sheep are as in Fig 8 and your dog is standing at your right side, then he will want to go behind the sheep in the shortest direction, which is to his right, anticlockwise. You must now use the 'Away to me' command to instruct the dog to go to the right. When the dog is standing on your left side (Fig 6) you will use the 'Come by' command to instruct your dog to go left,

clockwise. When you repeat these situations over and over again and keep giving your young dog the (correct) relevant commands, he will eventually begin to notice the difference in the command sounds.

Hand Signals

We try to use hand signals as little as possible, and advise you to do the same, preferring the dog to listen to the sound of the voice. Hand signals and body movement will give signals to your dog in the initial stages of training which will help to set him off in the correct direction, but you must be consciously aware that the 'finished' dog should be trained by voice or whistle sounds only: a dog which has to take its concentration from the sheep to

Come by. Lad is moving to his left (or clockwise) round the sheep trying to go to the opposite side of the sheep, so this is an ideal opportunity to give him the come by command.

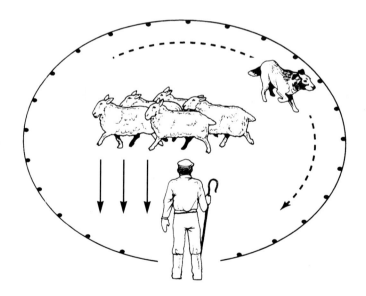

Fig 7 When the sheep are coming towards you, the 'come by' is still clockwise, that is, the dog moves to his left.

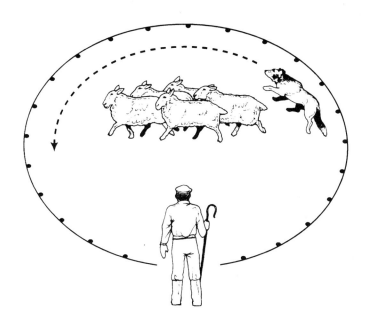

Fig 8   'Away to me' is the anti-clockwise movement of the dog around the sheep.

Away to me. Lad makes a good turn in an anti-clockwise direction (to his right) as he tries to restore the balance position with sheep between dog and handler.

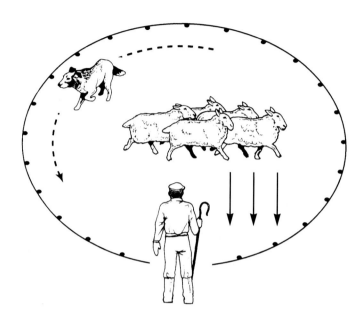

Fig 9 'Away-to-me'. Try to imagine that you are in the dog's head, so that you are sure the dog is moving anti-clockwise around the sheep.

look at the handler will lose its feel of the sheep, making its movement less fluent.

Whistle Commands

When you introduce whistle commands you must be sure that you are comfortable with the sounds you choose, for you need to be able to make the same sound each time. It is also worth considering your dog's attitude to work, because sharp whistles can make a dog run keener and would be ideal for a steady dog, whereas a lot of short, sharp, loud whistles may wind up a keen dog. Pick whistles that you like the sound of – there is no hard and fast rule. As a general guide, it is best to have a short whistle for one direction, a long sound for the other direction and a 'twiddly' one for the 'walk on'. If

you find it hard to understand the different kinds of whistle, listen to the birds, because some of the standard whistles are bird sounds. Examples to try are:

Command: right = 'away to me'
 Whistle = *'feeuwee'*

Command: left = 'come by'
 Whistle = *'fuuwi'*

Command: 'walk on'
 Whistle = *'pupi pupi'*

Practising Directional Commands

As yet it has been relatively easy for the young dog to guess which direction you

Lad is asked to go to the right (away to me). The handler is standing slightly in front of him, so that if Lad goes too straight, he will be able to push him out a little wider.

The problem with the round training pen is that the sheep are often too close to the side. Here the handler keeps alongside Lad as he goes around the pen to make sure that he does not cross in front of the sheep. Once the sheep move away from the side, Lad will be able to pass behind them more easily.

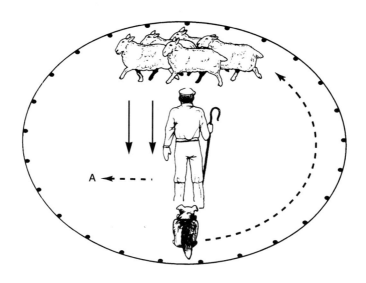

Fig 10   Teaching 'Away to me'. When the handler stands directly between the dog and sheep, the dog may circle the sheep in any direction. If the handler steps back to position A the dog will automatically go in the opposite direction

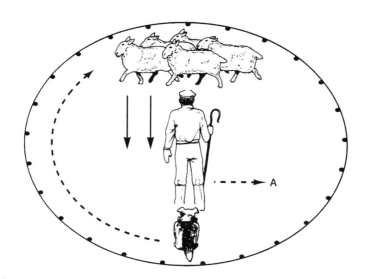

Fig 11   'Come by'. It is important that your dog enjoys both left and right out-runs – initially he may only want to go one way around the sheep.

want him to go : now is the time to make him think a little more. In Fig 10 when the handler is standing directly between the dog and the sheep, the dog will not be sure which way to flank, because the distance from the sheep each side is the same. Therefore if you step sideways to position 'A', then the dog should go to its right with the 'away to me' command. This situation will arise often, and it gives you the chance to see if your dog is listening to your voice or your movement.

Perhaps when the dog is lying directly behind you and you give him the 'away to me' (anti-clockwise) command, he will set off to the left. When this happens you must stop him immediately with a 'lie down' command; moreover it is important to watch your dog closely here, because the command to stop needs to be issued before he has committed himself totally to going the wrong way. Wait a second so he may realize that he is wrong, then move your position back in line to the direct centre of the sheep to your dog, and ask him to go to the right again. If he now goes the correct way, then allow him to go all the way round to the twelve o'clock position; if he continues to go in the wrong direction, then stop him quickly once more and move your position again slightly, and hopefully he will change his direction to go the correct way. Remember that the dog is responding to your movement before he hears the command, and also the motion of the sheep. Everything is interrelated, and as training progresses you must try to reduce your own movement so the dog listens solely to the spoken or whistle commands. Initially you can use both the voice and whistle commands at the same time as a basis of teaching, then gradually use one and then the other. You must always be encouraging your dog to listen to you, and you must train him to be ambi-

dextrous, that is, he must be able to go round the sheep on both sides.

Always allow the dog to 'hold' the sheep towards you for a short time before you manoeuvre to give another command. This will reinforce what you have already taught him, and he will relax again before you issue another instruction.

'Take Time'

A great deal of time can be spent on these initial training methods. In the long term it is beneficial that the young dog has a sensible approach to feeling the movement of the sheep, because this will help in work when a tricky situation arises. At this stage you are introducing your dog to a fluidity of movement around the sheep so that they always remain amenable to his movement. There will be times in the future when he is working in open spaces at a great distance from you, and you will then be confident that you have given him a sufficient foundation of knowledge to enable him to sort out any problems which may arise.

The Figure-of-eight Exercise

Your objective in the training pen is to achieve the figure-of-eight exercise: that is, to walk backwards inside the pen in a large figure-of-eight (as in Fig 13). You should try to do this with as little instruction to the dog as possible so that he turns the sheep away from the side of the pen, takes them across the centre and then turns them in the opposite direction at the far side of the pen.

Overcoming Problems

Many young dogs will circle round the sheep from only one direction in the early

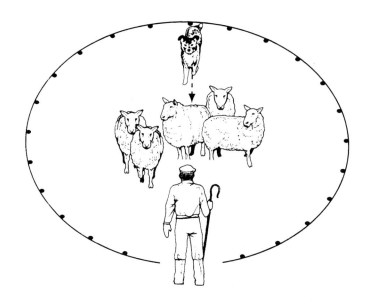

Fig 12   The dog learns to hold the sheep towards the handler in the balance position in a confident and relaxed manner. In between commands, it is good to allow your dog to hold the sheep towards you, as a constant barrage of commands builds frustration.

Lad wants to go in the wrong direction, so the handler blocks his path and asks him to go to his right around the sheep.

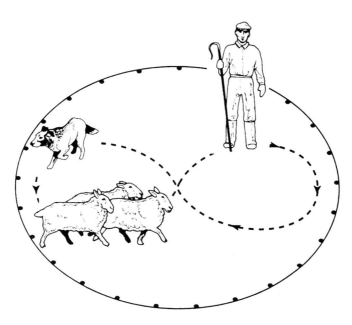

Fig 13   The figure-of-eight theory. The aim is to walk backwards in a large figure-of-eight with the dog always holding the sheep towards you. Then you will be sure that the dog can balance the sheep towards you and can circle the sheep in both directions

stages, and will cut back across the front of the handler if asked to go in the other direction. You must stop the dog and try to position yourself so that you are slightly forcing him to go in the direction he doesn't want to go. You must also be careful not to pressurize your youngster too much as he may 'freeze' and not want to move. Even if he runs through the middle of the sheep, as long as he is going in the direction you desire, don't discourage him; you must be patient with him, and eventually he will gain the confidence to go round *all* the sheep. And as he gains in confidence you can give him more difficult tasks, thus stretching his thinking abilities. Nevertheless, as soon as you feel that you are putting too much pressure on the youngster you must back off, and return to giving work that he can understand more easily. Then you can gradually build up again to stretch his mind a little further.

Working with the Different Types of Dog

The enthusiastic youngster will take more pressure from the handler because his desire to work the sheep is strong. He will create other problems by his speed of movement, however, and may upset the sheep every time he moves towards them. A dog of this temperament is often one step in front of the handler, seizing opportunities to harass the sheep, and the handler must therefore learn to think and react with more speed, as well as use firmer commands, without chasing around inside the pen.

When the sheep are balanced between the dog and the handler you can choose which way to move yourself; the dog will be sent in the opposite direction.

The careful worker will take very little pressure from his handler, and he will not be forced into situations he finds difficult. You must always encourage this sort of dog with happy-sounding commands; if there is no movement from the youngster at all, then it is your job to move the sheep into another position – just to stir them up a little bit to initiate movement from the dog. Also, the very careful worker should not be asked to lie down too much as he may want to stay down just watching; he needs to be encouraged to remain on his feet even when he is not moving forwards. A dog lying down and 'fixing' the sheep with a hypnotic stare will encourage the sheep to turn and stare back, giving you a 'no win' situation; whereas if the dog remains on his feet he is more of a threat to the sheep, the motion of his body preparing him to move forwards, rather than staying stationary. Teach your youngster the 'stand' command by gently pulling him to his feet with the lead and telling him to 'stand'; if he insists on remaining on the floor you can slide your foot beneath him and lift him to his feet with your toes (we must emphasize that you are only using your toes, and are not pushing or kicking him). You can also take advantage of every available opportunity of telling your dog what he is doing; so if he remains on his feet and *stands* behind the sheep, then fit the command to what he is doing and tell him to 'stand'.

By the time you have reached this stage in your training you should be building up a sympathetic rapport with your dog, vital for a good relationship.

CHAPTER 6

Training Outside the Pen

Once you are confident that your youngster has a good sense of feeling for the sheep inside the pen and you feel you have control of him, then the time has come to take the sheep outside the pen to see if he reacts in the same way. Sometimes, as a result of his new-found freedom a youngster will go back to chasing the sheep; if this happens then you may have to take the sheep back inside the pen to re-establish the training you have just done. On the other hand some youngsters will actually work better with more freedom because they feel restricted inside the pen and do not move as freely. When you first work outside the pen, try to let the youngster circle round the sheep holding them towards you; and every time they try to run away, allow him to go round to bring them back, so that they are turned and never have the feeling of escaping from him. This helps to settle them and they become more biddable, and the steadier the sheep, the easier it is to train your dog.

Establishing the Basics

Once again, walk backwards in a large figure-of-eight so that the dog makes turns from both directions. As the sheep settle, allow them to walk a greater distance from you so that your dog has a little farther to run to fetch them back. This is the start of the outrun training, increase the distance of the gather a little at a time. If the outrun is not complete and the dog cuts in or crosses in front of the sheep, you must move further into the field, reducing the distance between yourself and the sheep; you can now be reasonably confident that your dog will complete the outrun, because you are making sure that you are close at hand to rectify any mistakes.

Moving the Sheep from against the Fence

Allow your sheep to go close to, but not right against the fence, and then ask your dog to bring them back to you from a short distance. Most young dogs find it difficult to get behind the sheep to bring them when they are tight against a fence; they tend to cross in front of the sheep making it even more difficult for you to handle them, and creating problems the next time you ask for this manoeuvre. They may also run through the middle of the sheep because they are wary of going too close to them when they are adjacent to the fence. Our method is to reduce the distance gradually between sheep and fence as the dog gains confidence, making sure that the sheep are a sensible distance from the fence to begin with and then, as the dog becomes familiar with what is required of him and gains more confidence, moved nearer and nearer to the fence until the dog no longer has a problem with close and confined contact. Quite often when you enter the field the sheep will run to the farthest corner and wait until the dog comes round the outside of the field to fetch them. They may even defend their position in the corner, so it is vital that the young dog has the confidence to bring them away from that situation. If you do not feel that this is a good position to start from, then you must hold onto your dog, which should still be trailing a light line from his collar, and walk behind the sheep with him to move them out of the corner towards the middle of the field; in this way the start of your training will be much easier for him.

Establishing the Directional Commands

Now that your dog is happy being in the open field, always bringing the sheep back to you in a calm and confident manner, it is time to teach him to understand the left ('come by') and right ('away to me') commands more rigorously. Up until now we have accepted that he makes a few mistakes, just as long as he goes round the sheep and brings them back; moreover we have always asked him to go in the shortest direction, so it has been easy for him.

These powerfully built Swiss ewes can be moved by a small dog if they have the right approach. Odette Lieber's Maid shows a calm, positive method, which will be successful.

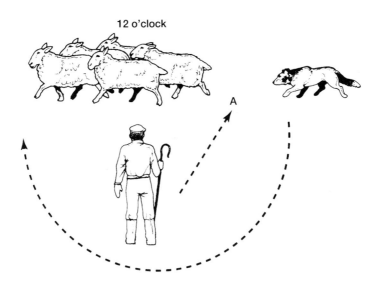

12 o'clock

A

Fig 14   Asking your dog to go in the opposite direction to his natural urge. By keeping the dog stopped and walking between sheep and dog, the handler can change to movement of the dog from 'away-to-me' to 'come by'.

Now we start to train him more extensively so that he is not able to guess in which direction we want him to go.

In Fig 14 any command from the handler will make the dog go to its right, to the twelve o'clock position. You have to remember that you have spent quite some time encouraging and developing your dog's instinct to hold the sheep to you, and he has no idea that you are now beginning a more advanced lesson; in his mind he is already committed to the right-hand command. But now you are going to ask your dog to come left, 'come by'. Watch your dog closely, because his body language will indicate what he is thinking and in which direction he intends to go; and should he move the wrong way, as soon as he does so stop him immediately, before he travels any distance and has therefore succeeded in going right to the left-hand command. Call his name in a friendly voice to try and draw his attention towards moving to you. To make it

easier, take a few steps forwards so you are going between the sheep and the dog, and ask him to 'come by' again. If he continues to go the wrong way, walk to a position nearer the line between him and the sheep, keeping him lying down. When you reach a central position your dog will slightly alter the way he is leaning (his body language informing you of his intentions again) and will then change the direction of his outrun to the other ('come by') side.

You must be encouraging when you draw your dog towards you, speaking to him in a friendly tone; you can bend down slightly, click your fingers or pat your leg – any of these will help to draw his attention away from the sheep and towards you. As he grasps this concept of coming towards you and flanking at the same time, try to use only the 'come by' or whistle command so that you are sure he is listening to you. In the initial stages the dog will nearly always circle round behind the handler, as in Fig 14.

When your dog does go in the direction you have asked for, you must allow him to circle all the way round to the twelve o'clock position; this is where he wants to be and you should never discourage him when he is learning. Only when you are sure he has grasped the concept can you teach him to stop before he reaches twelve o'clock. Make sure you keep teaching your dog to flank on both sides; what he is learning with his 'come by' he must also learn with his 'away to me' command.

Preliminary Training for Driving

Now we teach the dog to come in between the sheep and handler, as in Fig 15; make sure the distance between you and the sheep is sufficient for the dog to pass. Give the 'come by' command in a friendly voice to draw your dog towards you, and then move towards position 'A' (Fig 15) because this will encourage him to go in between you and the sheep. Initially he may be slightly confused as he reaches the mid-point between you and the sheep, and he may even still try to go behind you; however, do not pressurize him, just allow him to go all the way round to twelve o'clock. If he persists in going behind you next time, move towards the fence; when he realizes there is very little room for him to pass behind he will work out for himself to cross in front of you. Be patient with him, try to explain carefully to him where you want him to go, and eventually he will understand what is required of him.

It is not unusual for a young dog to grasp this idea in one direction more quickly than in the other. If you have major difficulties in teaching this to your dog outside the round pen, then go 'back to basics'. Outside the pen the sheep sometimes move away from the ideal position for you to train your dog – often just as you position him to teach him something new, they move and the command you were about to give is no longer relevant. By taking the sheep back inside the round pen you can easily set up an easier training position, until you both

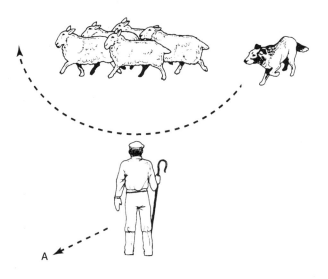

A

Fig 15   The dog circles the sheep towards the handler, but in front of him. If the handler walks sideways and slightly backwards at the same time, the dog will be drawn by his movement and a friendly command will encourage him to move towards the handler as he circles the sheep.

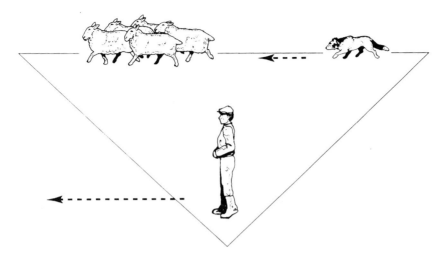

Fig 16   Driving the sheep begins with the handler walking alongside the dog so that the dog can see both sheep and handler in his field of vision.

become familiar with the commands and the positioning. Never be afraid to go 'back to basics'; repeating training steps which are familiar to both of you is a way of sealing the learning process.

Driving the Sheep Away from the Handler

So far all the training has been to educate the dog to bring the sheep back to the handler; now it is time to teach him to drive the sheep away. This is very difficult for a young dog to understand and so we must introduce such an unnatural concept gradually. We start as in Fig 16, with the sheep, and the dog and the handler forming the points of an equal-sided triangle, and in a quiet voice ask the dog to 'walk on'; if he wants to circle the sheep, stop him immediately and ask him again to 'walk on' – and you must adjust your position so that the triangular formation is reinstated. Every time the dog flanks or circles, stop him and ask him to walk on from there;

and of course, he now knows the 'come by' and 'away to me' commands, so you can reposition him to where he started from.

It is important to keep the triangular formation so your dog can see you out of the corner of his eye without losing his main focus of concentration on the sheep. As he walks, so the sheep move forwards, and so does the handler. Initially it does not matter if the direction of movement of the sheep is in a giant circle, because it is more important that the dog follows them in a steady and controlled manner. But as he begins to understand what you want, try to walk for longer distances so that he achieves a sense of purpose in taking the sheep in a particular direction.

The amount of time spent doing this exercise varies incredibly from one dog to another, some being much quicker on the uptake than others. However, it does not always follow that dogs which learn quickly will finish up the better dogs when training is finished. So if yours seems to be struggling a little to understand this exercise, be patient and persevere.

Driving begins with the handler walking alongside the sheep so that Kep has both sheep and handler in his vision, allowing him to concentrate always on the sheep. If he has to turn round to see where the handler is, he will lose his concentration on the sheep.

Driving the sheep away from you. Here the handler is using the stone wall as a block on one side so that it is easier for Kep to keep the sheep away from him.

Fig 17 Driving the sheep away from the handler. The handler stops walking alongside when the dog is driving confidently, so that the dog is allowed to take them forward on his own.

Once the dog has grasped the idea of driving the sheep along, the handler gradually moves out of the 'triangle' so that his dog is beginning to learn to walk in front and to drive the sheep on his own. This may only be for a few yards, but it is the start of driving longer distances. Initially your dog may look round to see where you are, and if this is the case you must walk alongside him again for a little while to give him more confidence before you stop and ask him to drive them away on his own once

Driving sheep with two dogs. Swaledale ewes with their lambs are not easy to manage, so the task is easier with two dogs. Pam and Kep drive the sheep down a steep bank into a new pasture.

more. Eventually he will learn to drive them right away, and by using the left and right commands he will realize that you want him to keep taking the sheep away from you without losing his concentration on them.

The Outrun and the Lift

The whole purpose of the outrun is for the dog to go round the sheep without upsetting them, and then bring them back towards the handler. The lift is the first contact of the dog with the sheep, and the initial reaction of sheep to dog can influence the whole aspect of how they will behave. This is why in trials ten points are awarded for the lift, because it is crucial to have a good, confident first contact with the sheep.

The Outrun

At the start of the outrun the dog should stand on the same side as the direction of running, within a couple of metres (about seven feet) from the handler. So if he is going on a right-hand outrun he should stand on the right side of the handler and not too far away from him. If your dog persists in running too straight on his outrun then you must stand between him and the sheep, and as he runs straight towards the sheep take a few brisk steps towards him shouting to him to go 'Out' – your movement towards him will be threatening, as will your tone of voice, and hopefully this will encourage him to change the direction of his outrun, making it wider. By repeating this each time he comes too straight he will learn that when you shout he is doing something wrong; even if he only slows down his speed, then he will not have the disturbing effect on the sheep that he first intended.

If your dog runs too wide, call his name in a quick, repetitive way and this will help to draw him in from the boundary fence. It is not ideal for a dog to be allowed to follow the fence all the way around the field; when he is working there may not always be a fence for him to follow, for example if he is gathering on a hill. Even if you will not be asking him to do hill work, often sheep may not be at the far end of the field, and it is time-wasting if the dog runs all the way round the edge unnecessarily. You are trying to teach your dog to run in the direction you want him to go, and so you must teach him to think about his own direction, to assess where you are trying to guide him, and how

Fig 18   Widening the outrun. A few brisk steps towards the dog as he runs straight for the sheep will encourage him to go on a wider outrun.

Tot Longton was a master at penning sheep on the trial field. These Rough Fell sheep at the Lake District trials test both man and dog to the limit before they will go in the pen. Mist waits for the next command before moving the sheep closer to the pen.

to relate this to his outrun to allow him to run behind the sheep at a sensible distance. Before you send your dog off on the outrun, it is a good idea to walk 5m (16ft) in the direction of the outrun with your dog in position ready to go. Ask your dog to 'see sheep': this is like a key word, and will indicate to your dog what is required of him, and the general direction of his intended outrun. Sometimes the sheep are not visible to the dog because of the contours of the field, and remember a dog's eyes are much closer to the ground than a human's. You must try to teach your dog to trust you as to where the sheep may be, so that he will run in the direction you ask even though they are not in sight. When you have gained his

confidence and his trust he will keep casting out in the direction you have sent him, and keep looking until he sees his sheep. If you aspire to run your dog at the International Sheep Dog Trials the sheep will be 800m (875yd) away, so it would be practically impossible for your dog to be able to see them from the start of the outrun.

The Lift

As we have said, the lift is the initial contact between dog and sheep. The ideal is for the dog to approach the sheep carefully yet confidently so that they turn and walk away from him. If the dog approaches hesitantly then the sheep will be apt to wait until he is very close, and they may even turn to challenge his authority, thinking he may not even have enough power to move them. On the other hand, if a dog approaches too quickly and abruptly, the sheep will scatter and run speedily away, and the dog will then start a helter-skelter-type chase of the sheep down the field, giving much stress to sheep and handler alike!

Handle Your Sheep Correctly

We cannot emphasize enough how important it is that sheep are handled carefully yet confidently; with correct handling they will settle to the dog, and be easily manoeuvred. On the farm, the sheep will be more content and easily managed when good dogs are used. Fast, stressful handling is no good for stock; and the stress caused is not only damaging to their life but also to the shepherd's profits. It is rather like a perfect circle: to keep your sheep content and free of harassment you need a good dog, to train your dog you need steady sheep. The use of the training pen in the early stages helps your sheep to become accustomed to your dog, and then you have to train your dog not only to work the sheep but to have a sympathetic feel for them. A Border Collie is a thinking dog, and the more you nurture his intelligence the better the end result and the more satisfying the partnership which you develop.

Teaching the 'Shed' and the 'Look Back'

By now you will have reached the stage where you can handle your dog quite adequately on the farm in a normal farming situation. At times, however, it will be useful to split the flock of sheep or shed them, to drive in two different directions, or to be able to send your dog back (the 'look back') to gather another flock, or stragglers from the first gather.

There is no substitute for work experience in the training of a sheep dog, and

The driving competition at the 1995 English National at Corby starts with the sheep at the post. Here Dick Roper's Cap, the English Champion, starts to drive the sheep for 400m in a straight line to the far end of the field.

ordinary everyday situations give both dog and handler new problems to deal with. It is good for the young dog to experience different jobs, both to widen his knowledge and increase his ability to think for himself, and it is an advantage to stretch his mind a little at a time, so that he gains confidence in his own abilities. However, never over-face him by giving him a problem that really only the most experienced dog can sort out; this is bound to give him a feeling of uncertainty and inadequacy.

So, in order to equip your dog to cope better with working situations, it is time to teach the shed (where the sheep are split into two groups) and the 'look back' (where the dog goes back for more sheep). Both can be trained at the same time, because the divided sheep are used to train the 'look back' command. Various situations can arise on a farm which involve shedding: if sheep were to escape from their field they could mix with another flock, and without a good shedding dog they would all have to be taken back to the farmstead to be separated. However, with the assistance of your trained dog you could gradually shed all the escapees from the flock and take them back to the field they should be in. And at lambing time, for instance, you may find you have a ewe which is having difficulty giving birth: however, no matter how great her problem, she will not want you to catch her, neither will you want to cause her unnecessary distress by chasing her round. A good dog will be able to assist you by focusing all his attention onto the single ewe, and will 'hold' her against a fence while you catch her. Lambing time again, and you may have given a ewe an orphan lamb which she resents: your trained dog will help you to 'hold' the ewe against the fence while the lamb suckles because his very

presence will arouse the mothering instinct in the ewe; and after a few days when the lamb has suckled enough milk for the ewe to detect her own scent, she will accept it willingly. In this situation the dog has to ignore all other sheep in the field and focus his attention on this single ewe, and this requires a great deal of concentration and confidence.

Teaching the Shed

When teaching shedding it is preferable to train on a larger number of sheep than when teaching the basics. You have spent a long time encouraging your dog to hold all the sheep together for you and he will find this new stage of his training confusing, and until he understands what you want from him it will only distress him if the sheep are constantly fighting to get back together. A small number of sheep will cling together for security, whereas a larger flock will separate more willingly, and this will allow you to show your dog what is required of him.

When the sheep are nicely settled in front of you, keep your dog lying down opposite the centre of them, and to begin with you do the work. Walk into the flock, splitting it in two, and encourage the sheep to walk in two different directions, creating a large gap between two small flocks. Bend towards your dog and encourage him to come to you with the 'that'll do' command. In the early stages of training you can forget about your sheep when you call your dog to your feet: keep your attention on him, and prevent him from developing the bad habit of trying to regather the flock as soon as he can. Remember, up until now your dog has always been trained to keep to the outside of the sheep, so calling him into the middle of the flock

It is easier to teach the shedding of sheep into two groups when there are a lot of sheep. Here the handler is asking the dog to come to him before holding the sheep. It encourages the dog to come towards the handler if the handler bends over a little, to give the dog more confidence to come in.

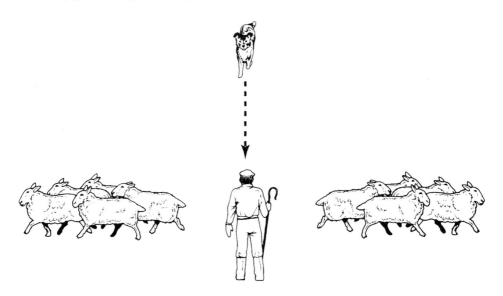

Fig 19   Shedding or splitting the sheep into two groups. Initially the handler himself works to make a large gap before he asks his dog to come in the middle of the sheep.

can be a mind-blowing experience for him; he will probably hesitate, looking both ways, and be severely tempted to chase after one of the packets of sheep. Nevertheless, it is important that your dog comes straight to you, and takes his attention off the sheep. Give him plenty of affec-

tion when he does come to you, and then allow him to regroup the two flocks.

After you have done this several times, and on different occasions, introduce an additional word to bring him through the sheep, as: 'that'll do, this'. The word 'this' can be a directional guide for him when he has learnt to shed, but at the moment you are putting emphasis on it, and it becomes an exciting sound encouraging him to come through with more speed. After several lessons he should be responding to 'this' and you will be able to drop the 'that'll do' part; although if an emergency arises when you are working, 'that'll do' is a reliable command to fall back on, to make sure he does not make a mistake.

Only when your dog is confident in coming between the two packets of sheep will you teach him to hold one away from the other. When he has gained this confidence call him through, making sure there is a large gap, and ask him to lie down between the two flocks. Now go round to the other side of the packet of sheep which your dog is facing (position A) and allow him to bring this packet towards you and away from the remaining sheep. If the sheep your dog is controlling try to break back to the others, encourage him to hold them to you and use the command 'this' so that he learns to cover any movement of

the sheep and holds them on his own. A dog's instinct makes him keen to learn and his reaction time is far superior to that of a human, so he will soon learn to hold the selected sheep to his handler, and will usually enjoy doing so.

The next stage is to reduce the distance between the sheep, so that the dog is confident of coming straight through the middle of them when there is only a small gap. The movement of the dog will cause the sheep to separate from each other, and the faster he comes in, the greater the impact he will have on his sheep. We think of shedding as an explosive command, the dog lying calmly on the other side, then suddenly rushing into the middle of the sheep with one single command 'this' and achieving a perfect shed with control and confidence.

Always stand facing the group of sheep that you want your dog to come onto and hold. He will soon learn your body language so that he will immediately come onto the ones you are aiming for. Try to make it a habit in the later stages of teaching the

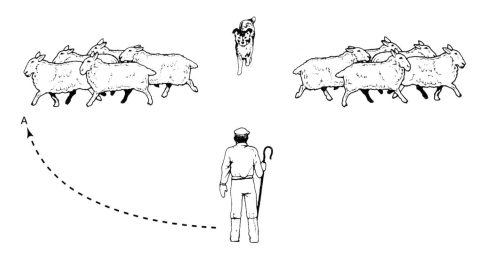

Fig 20 *Shedding and holding the sheep. The natural urge of the dog is to hold (or balance) the sheep towards the handler, so the handler moves his own position so that the dog can hold and balance one lot of sheep away from the other.*

Preparing to shed (or separate) sheep. The movement of the sheep draws Kep's attention. It is important for the handler to face the sheep that he wants the dog to turn onto.

Tweed, twice the English Driving Champion, knows exactly what is required when shedding. Here at the 1989 International, he is poised to take the last two mule sheep, and he only needs a small gap between the sheep.

shed to face the required packet of sheep and move slightly towards them, saying 'this'; not only will it be a good indicator for your dog which sheep you prefer, but it will help you to work together on what can be a difficult task in a work situation.

Not all dogs like shedding, and if they are slow to come in, do not try to force them or shout at them. They must enjoy coming through the sheep, otherwise they will sulk and persist in trying to join them back together, so it is important that you explain carefully what you want and that you exercise great patience; after all, you will be the one to benefit. Shedding should only be taught to a dog after it has reached a certain level of maturity; teaching them too soon in their working life may put them off for a long time, as their minds cannot cope with the added pressure. And if your dog enjoys shedding, be careful not to practise continually or he may soon begin to think he has to come through at the slightest gap and could end up shedding when you are trying to pen. Very embarrassing! Lastly, and on a more serious note, continually 'holding' young sheep which are fighting to get back together will either make your dog meaner or it will break his heart if they start to beat him. Months of careful training can be ruined by a moment's folly.

Stuart Davidson sheds off the last two Welsh ewes at the 1995 International trials, and allows the discarded sheep to drift away before taking the five remaining ones towards the pen and the Supreme title.

Shedding a Single Sheep

Undoubtedly this is one of the most difficult tasks that your dog will be asked to do. A single sheep separated from the flock will be very determined to return to the others, so your dog has to be 'up on his toes' to counteract every movement to stop it returning to the flock; the sheep may even try to jump over the dog in its effort to get back to its mates. Therefore it is essential that your dog is well used to shedding before he is asked to hold a single sheep.

To teach the dog to take a single sheep, hold the flock calmly in front of you as when shedding, then wait for an opportunity when one sheep at the end runs off alone. Before this sheep turns to rejoin the others the dog has to 'balance' with the handler and make a pincer-like manoeuvre so the sheep is forced to run in the opposite direction to the others, thus creating a gap the dog can run into. As he runs in when called, direct him immediately towards the single ewe; he focuses instantly on her and blocks her every attempt to return to the flock.

The singling of sheep is an exercise which must be used sparingly, because if the dog is constantly being challenged he may lose his patience and want to bite or

Kep counteracts the desire of a single sheep to return to the flock. There is no way that any handler can command his dog fast enough to control one sheep, so the dog's natural ability to balance on his own is a far superior method of holding one sheep.

Gem, the National Champion of 1992, shows what she liked to do most. She had superb balance when taking a single ewe, and they always turned away from her power.

grip the sheep in his frustration. Only the more mature dogs will have the confidence and ability to hold a single ewe – if you remain patient with a young dog and do not overface him, you will eventually have a mature, sensible dog able to single a ewe efficiently and with confidence.

Teaching the 'Look Back'

The 'look back' command requires the dog to turn round and go back for more sheep

Fig 21   The 'look back' command starts with the handler moving between the dog and the sheep that he is holding, so that his path to these sheep can easily be blocked. The handler then asks him to look back and go for the other lot of sheep.

and the teaching of this can be incorporated with shedding. When you have your flock split into two separate packets of sheep with your dog in between them, stand directly in front of the packet your dog is 'holding' so that you are between him and the sheep. Now you can ask your dog to 'look back' to the second packet of sheep. You may find it helpful if you raise your hands in the air to get his attention, for your aim is to divert his concentration from the flock he is holding and to the flock behind him, which should not have strayed too far away. If your dog continues to hold the closest packet of sheep, stop him with the 'lie down' command, then adjust your position so that you are blocking his path to the nearest sheep and try again with the 'look back' command. Your reaction to your dog's movement and the following 'lie down' command must be instant, for you are not going to allow him to move unless he is going in the direction you wish. Eventually he will realize that you are not going to allow him access to the first packet of sheep and he will begin to look elsewhere, and he should already have in his mind that there are other sheep in the field because it was he who released them from the flock.

When your dog finally understands you want him to go back for the other packet of sheep, do not worry if he goes straight after them; all we want initially is that he takes his attention from where he is , onto something else that is behind him. Gradually, as he becomes more accustomed with what is being asked of him, when he returns to collect the furthest packet of sheep he will give them more distance as he goes round them. As he gains in confidence, you can give him a left or right flanking command to ask him to go to a particular side of the sheep that he is

Look back. Kep has turned and returns for the sheep behind him. It is ideal if the sheep nearest the handler stand quietly, and the farthest ones are not far away but still easy to see.

Kep brings back the farthest pack of sheep to rejoin the nearest ones.

Fig 22   Once the dog understands that 'look back' means leave one lot of sheep and return for the others, the handler can move further away from his dog to give the command.

going back to gather; initially, however, give the flank command on the side that he is already running on.

When you are confident that your dog will look back and return for the second packet of sheep when you are stood in front of him, try moving to the other side of the flock that he is holding, and ask him to look back as he would in a work situation. The more confident he becomes with the 'look back' command, the more distance you can put between you, the

sheep and your dog, and as your training progresses you should be able to ask your dog to 'look back' when you are some considerable distance from the front packet of sheep.

Never underestimate the 'look back' command, for there will be times when you gather your sheep only to see more appearing behind the ones you have already gathered. With careful training of your dog there will be no need to bring the first packet of sheep to your feet before seeking to control the stragglers – with one command or whistle your dog will turn on his heels and at your direction will gather all the remaining sheep for you. To see your dog do this just once is well worth the training it takes. You may not even have a second packet to look back for to be able to appreciate the command, for if your dog is coming in too tight on his first outrun, he may be coming into the middle of the field too soon thus not collecting all the sheep. You can, and must, stop him as soon as he starts to move in, and give him the 'look back' command so that he takes his attention from where he is going and thinks in a bigger perspective.

You can also introduce a whistle command for the 'look back' if you wish, but it is not generally necessary, unless you are gathering in the hills. If you wish to achieve this, say the command and follow it with the appropriate whistle. Remember that this may need to be a little more complicated than any of your other whistles, as there must be no chance that your dog can misinterpret this whistle and think you have issued the 'look back' when you haven't. If you are gathering sheep from an open hillside where you will be continually redirecting your dog to collect more sheep, a 'look back' whistle can be far more practical than a verbal command.

Commands to Suit Everyday Work

As your training progresses you will be able to add more commands as you need them, and your everyday work will often dictate what you need. Perhaps your dog runs out a little too wide, in which case you can call his name and use the 'this' command to bring him into the middle of the field and closer to the flock. You may also find it an advantage to teach your dog a whistle command to hold the sheep apart after shedding has been completed, using a fast repetitive whistle. With a variety of commands and whistles you will be able to redirect your whole flock or part of it wherever you wish. Quite often not all the sheep are needed at once – maybe the pen will only hold half the total number of sheep you have – but with a well trained dog this will never be a problem for you. You and your dog will develop a seemingly telepathic working partnership.

The supreme test for a sheep dog is the International trial's final day, when twenty sheep are gathered from half a mile away. Here the 1995 winner Stuart Davidson has just finished shedding the five marked ewes and is now going to the final penning.

Now that you have an insight into training a sheep dog, it may be interesting to show you what these dogs are capable of throughout the working year.

Autumn

Autumn on a hill farm marks the start of the shepherd's year, as he introduces his carefully selected rams to his flock of ewes. Good rams are important, because it is on their merit that the quality of the following year's production of lambs largely rests. The sheep are gathered in from the hillside and this task may take all day, so the dogs must be in top condition. The ewes are separated into different groups so that each ram has its own small flock; with this selective mating the shepherd will know which lambs have been sired by which rams, so that at the end of the year a selection of new rams can be made for the following year. Coloured raddle is generally applied to the ram's breast, so that when he covers a ewe it leaves a tell-tale mark on her rump; and if it is changed to a different colour every week, the shepherd will know which ewes are due to lamb first in springtime. As each 'colour' group nears lambing, these ewes can be separated from the flock and brought into a pasture nearer to the farm for close observation. Every day in autumn the sheep have to be gathered and the raddle on the ram replenished or changed. The shepherd needs a good dog to hold the sheep close to the fence, because the rams will always try to avoid being caught. But this is a useful time of the year to take a young dog which has its basic training behind it, because the sheep are generally free-moving and respectful of the dog.

The sheep's cycle is every seventeen days, and starts when the daylight hours diminish; so the mating period is usually about five weeks long with any ewes which are missed on their first cycle being covered when they come in season again seventeen days later.

Winter

On a hill farm the ewes are turned back onto the open hillside for the winter, and they may have to be driven onto higher ground to prevent them from lingering around the foot of the hill waiting for the gate to open onto better pastures! The sheep dog will be expected to be able to drive the sheep back up the hill, where each family or group of sheep will have its own area on the hillside (its heft) where it grazes and spends most of its time, rather like a homing pigeon returning to its own place. In the autumn the ewe will return to her heft with her lamb and thus follow on the tradition.

During the winter months the sheep may be gathered in to be scanned, to ascertain how many lambs they are carrying. A contractor is usually hired to do this with a modern scanning machine, developed from the human version and which is generally very accurate. After scanning the shepherd will be able to segregate the ewes carrying single lambs from those with twins, or 'doubles'; better pasture is given to the doubles. The ewes carrying singles are more likely to be sent back to high ground until springtime, as they will be able to cope with lower feed intake levels; and every day the sheep dog will be expected to drive them back up the hillside.

In the event of severe snowfall, the flock may have to be gathered and taken from the high ground down towards the woodland where the snow drifts less. Sheep dogs seem to be able to work in any conditions, and if sheep are buried by a sudden snowfall then the collie dog, which has a good sense of smell, is often the first to find them.

Spring: Lambing Time

Ewes are carrying a heavy burden as they approach lambing time and are very susceptible to stress, and therefore the collie, which at other times has had to be firm and strong, must

Spot is forcing this Swaledale ewe to allow an orphan lamb to feed. The sheep knows exactly which are her own lambs and will constantly reject any others. After a few days, however, once the lamb has the milk from the ewe flowing through her, the ewe will take the lamb as her own.

now match his firmness with a certain amount of gentleness. Extra feed will probably be given to the ewes at this time, and it is amazing how their attitude to the shepherd changes when he enters the field with a bag of feed: all their past wariness disappears and the dog is no longer needed to gather them, because one rattle of the sack and they charge down the field, almost knocking the shepherd over! Once again a good collie will prove himself indispensable, to 'trough walk': he will walk in front of the shepherd clearing a space amongst the crowding sheep so the food can be evenly distributed either on the ground or in troughs.

Many people believe that your sheep dog should not be taken to the sheep at lambing time. We do not agree, and provided the dog is under control we feel it is beneficial to have him with you. The sheep soon become accustomed to the dog walking around them, and because he is calm and controlled, they do not run to the other end of the field. During the course of lambing there are bound to be ewes that require assistance in giving birth, and the dog will be on hand to hold the ewe in trouble in the corner of the field while you catch her; indeed, your dog will soon learn that he has to ignore all the other sheep and concentrate on one particular ewe.

The flock will be shepherded every day, and the task is so easy if you have a dog which will go round the outside edge of the field and remain under control. The shepherd who goes round his sheep in a vehicle may travel faster, but this way he may all too easily miss the vital tell-tale signs of trouble, because sheep grazing in a field will feel no threat from the 'mechanical dog' and will remain still, either continuing to graze or even lying down, and unless they move, albeit gently, the shepherd will not always be able to detect any problems. A shepherd walking round his flock with a quiet, sensible dog will cause the sheep to move: they will generally get to their feet and move slowly across the field, and as long as they are not pressurized they will spread out, enabling the shepherd to detect those in need of medical attention because they will be lingering at the back of the flock, as will a ewe in the preliminary stages of giving birth. With a fully trained dog not only can you detect casualties, but he will single out any ewe you need to inspect more closely so that you can catch it and administer medical care with little trouble.

Summer
During the summer months the flock will have to be gathered for worming, clipping, dipping and general inspection, all of which involves the sheep being handled in pens. It is amazing how some sheep dogs will react when they are in a confined space with sheep; some dogs that are careful and steady out in the open fields can change and become aggressive when working in pens. There is a closer contact with the sheep in this kind of work, and some may be tempted to try and 'headbutt' the dog; so a wise dog soon learns how to take care of himself in order to control the flock. If the dog is challenged by an arrogant ewe, then you should help him to face up to her, standing close by him and encouraging him to go forwards as he walks straight towards her, helping him to turn the ewe around. (Do not allow your dog then to take a 'cheap shot' at the sheep's backside, which is a cowardly thing to do.)

Kep holds the sheep and pushes them down the shedding race and through the footbath. The footbath is used to prevent the sheep from becoming lame. This chore is done regularly, so the sheep become accustomed to walking through the footbath.

Duck fashion! Fern (left) and Pam guide the ducks into the pen. Only one duck is out of line as they approach the entrance.

Gentle does it. Spot and Kep edge the Herdwicks ever closer to the pen. Using two dogs can be better because both sides of escape are covered.

Spot and Kep watch to make sure that the sheep do not escape from the pen.

Working Dogs Abroad

On reflection there is little a well trained Border Collie cannot do, and its capabilities often seem endless. If there are limitations they will probably not be apparent in this country; for example, the Kelpie in Australia has been trained to run along the backs of the sheep to the front of the pen, and then back down the pen on the ground, because it is this movement on the ground which encourages the sheep to move forwards. Kelpies and Huntaways are better suited to moving the massive flocks of sheep found abroad, although they fall short on the wide, sweeping outrun of the Border Collie.

The Overall Capabilities of the Sheep Dog

It must be remembered that a year on a hill farm will use practically every skill that a sheep dog has, but his capabilities also

Pam will work almost any animal, and here she waits for a command to fetch the deer. Little does she know how fast they can run!

(Inset) Fern has a gentle approach to the ducks, which is necessary to keep them calm.

include extensive and valuable work on lowland farms, and the dog trained for sheepwork also has all the basics required to make him good to work cattle. Although not all dogs will work both sheep and cattle and not all are suited to do both, the basic training described throughout these chapters will equip a dog for work of any nature.

As you work your sheep dog on the more practical aspects of shepherding, he will be gaining valuable experience as to how to handle stock; also he is subconsciously learning from you, as he helps you in each practical situation. And really there is no substitute for the experience your dog acquires from everyday working situations: building on a sound initial training, the dog will soon develop into the dog you are looking for, and you will be the one to benefit! Every shepherd has his own idea of what a good helper the dog can be, and he will always train his dogs into the system of work that suits him best. Moreover, a good trainer will always try to realize his dogs' full potential, and the more complete and comprehensive the training, the more the mind is stimulated, and the more satisfying the partnership.

Eric Halsall, second from the left, who has commentated on One Man and His Dog, *has been a great ambassador for the Border Collie through his regular reports on trials in the* Farmer's Guardian *newspaper.*

Preparing Your Dog for the Sheep Dog Trials

As the training of your dog progresses, you will be aware of how he improves in his method of working the sheep, and you may reach the stage where you will try to assess if he is capable of competing in a sheep dog trial. To work at trials standard, your dog will need to respond to your commands with greater accuracy than when working with a flock. At most trials, especially in the north of England, you will only be working on three sheep, and this requires a great deal of extra 'polish' from your dog. At home you may think you have good control of him and that he has command over his sheep, but when you go to a trial the field is different, the sheep may not be the same breed, and the whole environment will be strange. This can be mind-boggling for the dog, so be prepared for a few hiccoughs when you run him somewhere different; it is always an advantage if you can go to a friend's field and practise working him in an entirely strange situation. Usually he forgets almost everything you have taught him, a temporary memory loss which can prove very embarrassing! Furthermore, working a dog at a sheep dog trial can be a nerve-wrecking experience for the handler, and this nervousness will be sensed by the dog and he will quickly take advantage of the situation. However, if you don't expect too much, you won't be disappointed.

Polishing up your Performance

To put more 'polish' into your dog's training it is a good idea to go back through the training procedures, so that he is absolutely confident of your commands. His reactions will have to be swift and positive, and the 'stop' command must be instant. It can be very exciting for a young dog to see a few flighty sheep running away down the field and you must be able to control his desire to chase after them, which in the early stages may be insatiable. But if your training has been successful and your dog works sensibly, there will be a great deal of satisfaction gained by working him on a trials field. You will be able to compare and compete with him against others of a similar standard that are working on the same day, and enjoy the satisfaction of completing your first run with a dog you have trained yourself.

During your training or in your everyday work, try to imagine that you are walking out to the trials post. Your dog will have to learn to trust your judgement, for there will be times on the course that he will not be able to see sheep, or worse, he may watch the previous competitor take his sheep to the exhaust pen, and it can be difficult for him to comprehend that there are more sheep waiting in the distance. He will need to outrun efficiently and come in to lift his sheep sensibly – don't wait until you are competing to watch him do everything correctly on the wrong packet of sheep! Create a situation on your home ground where he cannot see sheep, and when he must learn to trust your command.

At the end of the outrun on the trials field there may be two or three people 'holding' your sheep near the post, and if your young dog has not come across this situation before it may get upset. This can result in him being too shy to go around them; he may even cut across the front of the sheep and his instinct could make him hold them to the people at the top of the course instead of bringing them to you. Try to create a similar situation at home so that he will be more confident on the trials field. If you have no-one willing to stand in the field while you train your dog – and not everyone can be expected to share your enthusiasm! – deputize some scarecrows! A hat and a coat on a post should be enough to give your dog an idea of what is expected of him.

National Trials Courses

Although trials courses will vary throughout the country, they usually follow a similar format. Open trials for more experienced dogs are obviously more testing than nursery trials, which are for the less experienced, where the course tends to be smaller and easier to encourage the younger dogs.

Outrun, Lift and Fetch

The outrun is worth twenty points and the dog must go round the sheep, giving them plenty of room. Then they have to 'lift' the sheep, which means setting them going in a careful yet confident way: it is worth ten points, and will influence the rest of the run. On the fetch the dog should flank left and right freely, trying to keep the sheep on a straight line between the lift point and the fetch gates and then on to the handler. The sheep are then turned round the handler and set off on the drive which is normally triangular. The direction of the first drive will vary from one trial to another. The shedding and singling of sheep tends not to be done in nursery

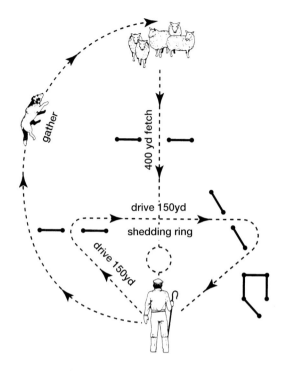

Fig 23   A national-style course.

trials, being introduced when the dogs have more experience.

Penning

Penning sheep with a dog on a trials course is not an easy task, because the dog has to be able to balance and hold the sheep every time they want to break away from the pen. Having said that, each time he goes to a trial the handler will gain more experience: he will learn where to stand, and how to keep his dog in the correct position to hold the sheep towards the gate of the pen. The dog has to hold the sheep gently but firmly so they eventually realize that the pen is the only place they can go: if he is too careful the sheep will realize and become cheeky, thus trying to outmanoeuvre him; too strong, and the sheep will chase round and round the pen, never settling in a position to be put into it.

Tweed holds the four ewes at the famous old trials at Longshaw. One of the features at the trials is a large clock, which is there for all to see. There is little chance of winning the spoils if the course is not completed in the allotted time.

The shedding race. In some of the European trials, practical work has to be done. This is Erica Sommer with her dog Flocky. Flocky holds and pushes the sheep into the race while Erica sheds off the marked sheep.

Shedding and Singling

Shedding and singling of the sheep are worth ten points each, and may have to be conducted in a circle (shedding ring) marked with sawdust heaps. With the sheep held between them, the dog and the handler will form a partnership, making small movements to encourage a gap to form in the tiny flock where required; the dog should then 'explode' into the gap, holding the designated sheep apart from the rest. Sheep under duress in the shedding ring will cling closely to each other, so it is essential that this part of the trial is conducted as calmly as possible. The shed or single is required to meet a certain standard on the trials field, and the judge will generally indicate if your effort has been conducted satisfactorily.

Knowing the Course

It is advisable to check with the course director or clerk as to exactly what is required on the course, for there is nothing worse than having a quality trial with your dog and then being told that you have gone the wrong way on the drive. Although most drives are similar, the actual difference from one trial to the next could make all the difference to a winning run. If the sheep have not been specially marked, many judges will usually ask for the last sheep to be singled: this means that the dog has to come on towards the last sheep's head, instead of chasing it off from behind. Failure to complete the course could result in a good run receiving lower points than expected; so always make sure you are familiar with the course before you stand at the post.

Sheep dog trials are primarily designed to test the working ability of the dog in everyday situations, and each part of the course relates to some task done on the farm. However, as you are working small numbers of sheep at a trials, your dog has to be more careful, more flexible and more patient than he would need to be with a large flock at home. Many a local farmer will watch a trial and say. 'My dog could have done better than that one!' The answer is, and always should be, 'Go and get him, then, and let's see him perform!' They seldom take up the challenge, because it is never as easy as it appears to be!

Working your sheep dog at a trial shows that your dog can adjust to working with varying types of sheep, varying weather conditions and different terrain. But remember, the first time your dog competes on a trials field there are bound to be more problems than being on a field at home where he knows where everything is.

The Handler's Attitude

It is important for you to have the right mental attitude. When you compete at your first trials with your dog, do not expect too much, and don't be disappointed if you do not make the prize list. The only thing to worry about is how your dog worked: there are plenty of excuses for things going wrong, but if he works well, takes all your commands and shows good common sense, then you can be satisfied. The first few trials you go to are really a training ground for subsequent trials, and there are no short cuts to success on the trials field; you have to 'pay your dues' by travelling with your

dog, and increasing his experience and confidence as you go. Don't take any risks by asking him to do something of which he is not yet capable; you must gradually stretch his ability to cope with more difficult situations. And if he continues to work well at home as well as on the trials field, then a prize will come your way eventually. Moreover, on the first occasion that you win a prize at a nursery trial with your own dog which you have spent months training, you will surely experience the most fantastic feeling of well being there is. The standard of sheep dog trialling has increased so much in the last few years that you can be quite sure that you will not be given a prize unless you thoroughly deserve it.

Even if you never obtain the level required to reach trials standard, it gives great satisfaction to have a dog working well on the farm. Some dogs are just not cut out to be a trials winner: they may not like travelling, or they may not have enough patience, or they may even have too much! However, the trials field is the only way to compare dogs working in similar conditions, so just have a go if you want to – but be sure to enjoy whatever happens.

The Maltese cross. Some trial courses include this feature as a test of shepherding. The sheep may have to be taken both ways through the race. Here Gem takes the sheep around one end of the Maltese cross.

CHAPTER 7

Problem Solving

A Dog that Does not Want to Work

Depending on his age, there may be a variety of reasons why a dog does not want to work. It is possible that he is not psychologically mature enough: his actual age has nothing whatsoever to do with this, and some dogs of eight months old can be more mature than others of eighteen months. Even litter brothers and sisters do not always develop at the same pace, so although your dog may be one year old it does not necessarily follow that he is mentally adult enough.

Maybe he is not yet ready for work: in this case you must give him time to mature, because you will never force a dog to work. Try to stimulate his instinct by moving sheep around close to him, and encourage him with 'shushing' sounds when he moves near to them. Never try to force him to work, and if he chases the sheep, allow him to do so until he gains his confidence. Often something will stimulate his desire to work – a cat or a rabbit moving suddenly in front of him will instigate the desire to hunt or chase. Do not try to hold him back too soon when he does show some interest: only when he begins to show some desire to work and appears to be enjoying his time moving sheep around should you issue a 'lie down' command.

Some dogs just do not want to work at all, and will usually be much happier as a non-working companion for someone; but don't give up hope until you are certain. However, usually if a dog is over two years old, time is running out for it to mature enough or to gain interest, and your time may be better spent with a keener youngster.

A Dog that Refuses to Stop

The most common reason for a dog refusing to stop is that the handler has been in too much of a rush to have him working. Probably not enough time was spent on his basic training without sheep in the first place, for without this initial training you cannot lay a sufficiently solid foundation for your dog to be biddable when he is excited by the prospect of sheep running. The only solution is to go back to the beginning with your training and teach him to stop when he is on a long, light line without any sheep present. Do not be tempted to try him again with sheep until you have an instant stop from him, because if he is not willing to listen to you outside the sheep field, you have little chance in it. The 'stop' is one basic lesson you cannot afford to rush.

Another possible reason may be that the dog thinks that the 'stop' command is a punishment. If at some time he has been doing something wrong and to correct him he has been told to stop and you have then shown your displeasure with him, he will

The winter gather has to be done whatever the weather is like. Here the dogs hold the sheep towards the fold after being brought down from the snow-covered slopes in the Trough of Bowland.

associate the command with unpleasantness. Shouting at your dog continuously will also make him unwilling to stop: there should be no need to shout at him to stop him if you have educated him correctly during his basic training, and if he associates a raised voice with displeasing you, shouting the 'lie down' command will only serve to confuse him. Go back to teaching him that the stop command is a 'happy command' and that he will be praised for correct behaviour: thus, when working with the sheep, he will always be happier to stop at the balance position (twelve o'clock). Try to ensure that the sheep are settled and help him to keep them 'balanced', encouraging a 'happy stop' position for a few lessons until he realizes he is not going to lose his sheep by stopping and that he is pleasing you.

A Dog that Runs too Fast

Very few young dogs start out by running in a slow, controlled manner and the more inexperienced handler may feel that the dog is running too fast. Everything can happen very quickly when a young dog has his first few lessons in the sheep field, and the novice handler who has a lot a to remember, can very easily be intimidated, for his reflexes are not as spontaneous as those of the more experienced handler.

Experienced handlers cope more easily, and positively enjoy the speed of the dog's movement which will be invaluable in future aspects of work, if correctly used. Ideally we like a fast outrun, and quick responses on the flanking movements. The speed of the dog can mesmerize the sheep if used properly, and they soon realize there is no chance of escaping in any direction – although a fast-running dog can have an unsettling effect on the sheep if it is allowed to run too close, so it has to be made to run a little wider than the slower dog. If the 'stop' command is spontaneous, the sheep can be allowed to move away before another movement from the dog is allowed; if not, a helter-skelter type of action of the sheep will result because the more the dog pushes on to the sheep the faster they will run, and the faster they run, the keener the dog will be to keep up with them.

It is important that the handler uses strong and clear commands, and makes the dog wait between each command so that he is obliged to learn a little patience. If you are continually commanding your dog without making him wait, he will constantly be expecting to be on the move; he must learn to wait and to listen. Never try to outrun your dog, unless you are 100 per cent certain that you will reach the sheep before he does. Linford Christie is probably one of the few people who could achieve this, and most dog handlers won't stand a chance – they will end up just chasing their dog, which will only encourage it to run even faster! Far better to make sure your sheep are quiet, a necessity for training a fast dog, and then make him go wider by trotting round in between him and the sheep; he will go in a bigger circle and will soon realize that he cannot get to the sheep before you do.

A Dog that will only Outrun in One Direction

Sometimes when a dog doesn't want to go the way you have asked he will cross over on the outrun. Quite often a dog will prefer to outrun on one particular side, something which should be overcome in the initial stages of training, but it is also possible that the direction of the movement of the sheep may cause the young dog to cross his course in order to reach his destination sooner. The terrain may also cause a young dog to lose his outrun or cross his course: rough or undulating

ground can make him lose sight of his sheep, and this will confuse him, and upset his sense of direction.

To try to solve this problem, go back to the 'figure-of-eight' movement with the sheep when they are close to you, making sure that your dog flanks willingly in both directions before asking him to work further away. When you feel confident he is listening to you, allow the sheep to drift away 20m and then ask him to outrun on the side he doesn't like. Make sure you stand between him and the sheep so that if he wants to cross in front of them or come in on his outrun, then you are already in a position to tell him to go out. Keep increasing the distance gradually so that you are always confident that he will stay on the same side he sets off from. Another factor may be the lie of the land: if you put your sheep at the other end of the field you can assess your dog's outrun when he is casting in a different direction.

A Dog that Eats Manure or Grass as it Works

Some dogs have an irritating habit of picking up sheep droppings or grass while they are working. The first thing to check is their diet: could there be a possible vitamin deficiency, and have they been wormed regularly? However, the most likely cause of this problem is stress, or pressure from the handler, and the more pressure the handler puts on the dog, the more likely it is to pluck at the grass! The handler must therefore try to minimize this feeling of stress by praising the dog more, and allowing him to do more of his work on his own, with fewer commands from you – he has to learn to relax and to enjoy his work; it doesn't matter if he doesn't achieve perfection – it is more important that he works sensibly and confidently. It is very easy to cause a dog stress without realizing it; for example, if you have been having a problem with your training and suddenly your dog begins to respond, it is a temptation to carry on for too long and to push him too far – it is much better to walk out of the field when he is at his best, leaving him with a good memory.

It may take much more time to reach a top level of achievement with a dog showing this type of behaviour.

A Dog that Likes to Pull Wool as he Flanks

A dog that grips sheep as he flanks round them can be showing a sign of weakness, not power; it is a very cheap trick for him to pull wool out as he circles the sheep. You will need to know how much discipline your dog will endure in order to stop this habit – but stopped it must be because it can be very difficult to correct if it goes on for a long time.

Take your dog back into the training pen and set up a situation where you are sure he will want to grip. As he comes in to take wool, or better still just before – and you can often tell when he intends to do so by the look in his eyes – shout in your loudest voice 'No!!' Don't worry what happens as long as he does not grip. Allow him to run as close as he likes or as fast as he likes, but shout 'No' every time he opens his mouth to grip. Moreover, you must make sure that you prevent your dog from gripping by always staying close to him, and letting him know that you will intervene if he doesn't listen to you. It may also be an idea to take him into a pen with many sheep milling around so that he cannot focus his attention on any particular one;

though once again, make sure that you stay close to him.

If your dog continues to grip when you are shouting in his ear – remember, do not use the 'lie down' command, because this must remain a happy command – then more severe measures may have to be used. So, to get his attention, try shaking an empty plastic bag close to his ears, along with a shout of 'No' just as he pulls on the sheep.

A Dog that Refuses to Walk up to Sheep

This shortcoming may be the result of hereditary tendencies, or it may be that the dog is unsure of himself. It is very easy to accuse a dog of being short of power, but it may be that he is uncertain of coming forwards, and possibly he has been instructed to stay off his sheep. Nevertheless, it is an embarrassing experience if you have to walk down the field at a trial to bring the sheep with the dog because he had not got either the confidence or power to lift them on his own. To help him gain confidence, you will have to go back into the training pen and encourage him to come forwards. This is best achieved when you are close to the sheep yourself, because if they try to 'stand him off' and he is having difficulty moving them, you can then help him to turn them, giving him the confidence he may be lacking. Move around excitedly yourself to encourage your dog to do the same; once he has gained the confidence to move the sheep, he will remember in future. Allow him to run close behind them, and don't even discourage the occasional grip; he will learn after a while that this is not necessary.

If, after all your efforts, the dog still does not want to move the stock, then provided he is over two years old, you might try taking him into a very confined pen with the sheep. They may want to be aggressive towards him, making him feel thoroughly cornered, and this can encourage him to 'stand his ground'; but this should be considered as a last resort when all else has failed. The result will be that the dog either sinks or swims, in other words he learns to fight, or he submits totally and becomes a lapdog.

A Dog that Looks Constantly at its Handler

This problem is usually the result of too much training of a mechanical nature. The training of a sheep dog is comparable with a painting: when it is finished you don't see all the individual brush strokes, more the picture as a whole. It is also because the dog has become unsure of himself, and therefore constantly referring to his handler for his next command; he simply does not have the confidence to make a decision on his own. You must therefore make a conscious effort not to wave your arms or crook, because this will distract your dog's mind from the sheep. Try to reduce your own movement, and also the number and volume of your commands, so that your dog has longer periods when he can concentrate solely on the sheep. He does not need to be looking at you but he must learn to listen. Remember that a dog's ears are much more sensitive than ours, and it is not always the case that he has closed them!

A Dog that Flanks Squarely or Too Wide

The term 'square' or wide flanking is often believed to be the ideal movement around the sheep. It conjures up the notion that the dog has to move at right-angles to his stock, although this is not what is meant by the term. However, when you are on a hillside it is no use trying to control flighty sheep if your dog is flanking too wide: sheep will realize that he is too far away to be in command of them, and they will almost certainly change direction and escape the other way, with the dog powerless to catch them. The dog that flanks too wide will completely lose contact with his stock and often the direction in which they are running

Your dog must be kept closer to his stock so that he makes a rounded flank each time, and always keeps a 'feeling' for the sheep; call him by using his name in a quick, friendly tone, or quicken up your whistle sounds to speed him up so that he is less likely to flank too wide. However, every dog tends to have its own 'comfortable' distance of working from sheep, and it isn't easy to alter this distance, especially when the sheep are moving very fast.

A Dog that Circles (or Heads) the Sheep when Driving

If your dog drives the sheep happily for short distances but then goes round and brings them back (heads them) this is nearly always because you are guilty of having pushed his training too quickly. Go back to the basics of being alongside your dog while he is driving in long straight lines until he regains his confidence. Then start allowing him to take them alone, and if you feel he is on the point of heading them, move forwards yourself and reduce the distance between you. Sometimes call him back to you, leaving the sheep to drift onwards up the field; this will prevent him from concentrating on them to the exclusion of listening to your requirements. If you vary your methods you will keep him thinking.

To Sum Up

- There are bound to be problems whilst training a sheep dog. However, no pain … no gain is a very apt saying, for at the end of the problems it is so very rewarding to see him improve by your instruction alone. So if your dog seems to be having trouble, you must try to step back, metaphorically speaking, and try to assess what it is and how you can help him.

- Don't be frightened to go back to the basics when training. Many handlers on training courses think their dog is more advanced than it really is, so take time and care with your training; there are no short cuts, and there is no particular formula that will suit every dog.
- Always try to see the whole picture as you are progressing; moreover, the dog may see things differently to you, so try and stay one step in front of him.
- Enjoy your dog and his work; there is a special feeling when things go well and everything inside learns to relax. Every dog can be trained to a certain extent, and it is up to you to reach his maximum potential.

Good Luck!

Alone on the hill. Kep scans the horizon to see where the sheep are. He knows it is a big task to gather the fell and take them down to the homestead below.

CHAPTER 8

Sheep Dog Trials and the ISDS

Introduction to the International Sheep Dog Society

The first recorded sheep dog trials were held in Bala, North Wales, in 1873, but it was not until thirty-three years later that the International Sheep Dog Society (ISDS) was formed, following a meeting of English and Scottish sheepmen in 1906. Shortly afterwards the first International Trials were held in Gullane, Scotland, and except during the war years they have continued to be an annual event.

Now, almost a hundred years later, the ISDS has over 6,000 members from all over the world, not just from the obvious places of sheep concentration such as Australia and New Zealand, but also from the Americas, South Africa, the Falklands, Scandinavia, the Middle East and the continent of Europe, to say nothing of a growing interest in Japan! Each year sees quite a few of our overseas members in the UK as spectators at our National and International Trials. They come, not only to see the finest dogs in competition and to learn from their handlers, but also to assess the dogs' ability for their own requirements 'back home' – wherever that may be – and then seek to buy the dogs, or more specifically their progeny. The UK is very much

the 'kennel of the world' as far as the working sheep dog is concerned.

The ISDS was founded with the intention of stimulating interest in the shepherd and his calling, and to secure the better management of stock by improving the shepherd's dog. This is still the intention today, for without a good working dog the work of the shepherd, both on the hills and the lowlands, would be impossible. One good dog can do the work of a dozen men, as the shepherd is the first to testify. Indeed, British agriculture owes a tremendous debt to these hard-working collies, and all too often perhaps their efforts and praise remain unsung – but they are never underestimated! So the constant improvement of these dogs is a prime requirement. To help facilitate this, in 1955 the society produced its first stud book in which pedigrees had been researched back to the early 1900s, commencing with the famous Old Maid. Today, the pedigrees of over 6,500 puppies continue to be registered each year, and the stud book of the ISDS is the principal work of reference concerning such pedigrees in the world. It is therefore invaluable for those serious breeders who seek excellence in the working sheep dog, conscious of the part that pedigrees play in enhancing the skills of the breeder and assisting him to produce better and better dogs.

The Role of Sheep Dog Trials

The culmination of the breeder's skill is demonstrated in Sheep Dog Trials, and although breeding is of paramount importance, it is the Sheep Dog Trial that is the 'shop window' for the end result of the breeder's labours, and is the endless delight of those who compete and those who spectate. Competition is held between the 'home' nations of England, Ireland (including the Isle of Man), Scotland and Wales. To be eligible to enter a National Sheep Dog Trial the dog must be entered in the society's studbook before the 1st June in the year of that trial. National Trials are run over a 400m course, using five sheep and with the standard elements of Outrun, Lift, Fetch, Drive, Shed Pen, Single. From these National Trials, the fifteen highest-placed competitors meet together in competition in the International Trial. At the International, the same size of course and number of sheep is used for the Qualifying Trial which is run over the first two days, and then on the third and final day, the most coveted title in the sheep dog world is contested: that of Supreme Champion! For this competition, the course is lengthened to 700m, with a double 'lift' and a total of twenty sheep are piloted around the course. This is the greatest test any working sheep dog can possibly undertake, and the 'Supreme Champion' may be justifiably proud of his accolade.

As far as possible, sheep dog trials follow the conditions and work to be encountered in everyday shepherding on the hills and farms of the UK. They are not intended as a succession of 'tricks' or gimmicky obstacles, but rather hope to offer a practical

Snowdonia, which is typical sheep country in Wales, where sheep dogs are an essential part of tending the flocks.

*Tot Longton and Jess, and Thomas Long-
ton and Bess are all Supreme Champions. It is very rare to have two dogs from
the same farm to achieve so much.*

*(Below) Double-doubles. From left to
right: Tweed, Fern, Gem and Pam have
all twice been English National Brace
Champions. Tweed and Gem were
superseded in time by Fern and Pam.
Here they all move in unison to hold the
sheep against the stone wall.*

demonstration of the skills the dog uses
every day of his working life. The dogs you
see on the trials field are not kept specially
for the sport by their masters: those same
dogs will have been at work, probably that
very morning before setting off for the trial,
and it is true to say that the skills they
acquire in their everyday work are essential to help them gain maximum points.

The system of scoring at trials is that a
maximum number of points is allocated
for each element, and dog and handler
actually 'lose' points for any faults as they
progress around the course. The whole of
the trial is of a practical nature, and the
ISDS rules for these competitions are
solely concerned with the working capabilities of the Border Collie and its master.

There has been tremendous interest and
following of the sport of Sheep Dog Trialling,
enhanced no doubt by the success of the television coverage it has attracted over the
years. The only individuals not affected by
this comparatively sudden 'recognition' are
the dogs – often referred to as 'the wisest
dogs in the world'. They remain unspoiled

Bess, having just won Supreme title, cannot understand what all the fuss is about and would much rather get back to work. There is a very special feeling between a man and his dog, which is necessary to reach the top.

by the fame of their ability and of their handlers, and it is this unaffected joy in the work that they do that gives trialling its charm.

The International Sheep Dog Society has this highly apposite ancient motto:

There is no good flock, without a good Shepherd – and there is no good Shepherd without a good dog.

Sheep Dog Trials Today

For more than a century shepherds have enjoyed the challenge of sheep dog trialling, competing against other dogs and handlers, and demonstrating their handling skills and the capabilities of their dogs over courses designed to test their expertise in most aspects of work. At one time trials were attended by competitors, families and friends and a few locals, but as the years passed and the Border Collie's popularity has progressed, so sheep dog trialling has become more of a spectator sport. The winter nursery trials are staged to give young collies an introduction to trialling, and usually have little to offer spectators other than the enjoyment of watching the sheep dog at work. Often held in inclement weather, these trials are organized with the dogs and handlers in mind rather than the spectator, and as the

Working in tandem. Tweed (left) and Gem, twice National Brace Champions, balance the sheep between them as they fetch them down the field.

dogs are of only novice status, there is often little to hold the attention of all but the most enthusiastic follower. However, during the summer months when the dogs are more experienced and the trials are of Open standard, the spectator can enjoy not only good competitive trialling, but stalls offering refreshment and a variety of side stalls, all of which provide something for the whole family.

Enthusiastic spectators and would-be handlers are prepared to brave all kinds of weather to learn a little more about the sheep dog and trialling, and there is much more to working a dog and competing at a trial than many people first realize. Each trial depends for its very existence upon the sheep being provided, and if they are not 'on site' someone has to transport them, hurdles and pens also have to be provided and erected, and of course every trial has to have a judge. The competitors will often have been up at dawn attending

to their normal chores before travelling to the trial, and as venues are often few and far between, what is local for some may mean a 200- or 300-mile round trip for others. There can be little doubt as to the almost magnetic appeal of the trials field when it is considered that a competitor's run with each dog will only last for approximately 10 to 12 minutes, that most trials allow no more than two dogs for each competitor (and many competitors only have one dog, but still travel miles to compete) and that if luck is against them they may not even complete one or either of their runs, yet time and again they compete, enjoying the good runs and learning from the not-so-good ones. And each time a dog proves its worth by gaining a place in an open trial, it takes its handler nearer to being qualified to compete at a National Trial and then maybe a chance to represent his country at an International Trial.

The English team of 1995, which was selected at the trials at Corby, held in extremely hot conditions.

The Judges

If the days are long for the competitors, they must seem even longer for the judges because not only do these stalwarts have to tend to the needs of their own stock before leaving home to judge the trial, but they will be amongst the first on the field and the last to leave. Judging is not an easy task, and often what to the novice spectator or handler seems a not very competent run, may in fact have been one of the most skilful of the day, only appearing less due to a group of very wilful sheep. It is important that the judge watches every second of each run and judges each dog according to its own merit. Not all dogs will have the same outrun: some may run wider than others, and sometimes they may need to work at a greater distance from the sheep than they do from others. Some lie down, and some prefer to remain standing when told to stop; some have plenty of 'eye', others little. The judge has to take all this into consideration, how the dog works, its effect on the sheep, and of course the end result.

To understand a little about judging makes spectating at a trial more interesting. The ISDS stages judging seminars, where members can learn or improve their judging skills or simply gain more knowledge for when they next attend a trial.

Judging a trial at Littleborough takes all day. Raymond Wild stretches his legs in the sunshine but continues to watch the competitor at the post, John Harvey with Sue.

National and International Trials have always enjoyed a large spectatorship, but as people become more aware of the skills of these intelligent working dogs, the smaller trials now also attract enthusiastic followers. The popular television series *One Man and His Dog* has done much to promote the working Border Collie, not only by bringing the sport right into people's homes, but also by carefully guiding viewers through each stage of the trial; this has helped to increase their knowledge of some of the finer points of trialling and judging. One of the commentators responsible for guiding viewers through the intricacies of trialling in the earlier series of *One Man and His Dog* was the late Eric Halsall, not only well known for his explicit and enthusiastic commentary but also a highly respected member of the sheep dog fraternity, having spent many years dedicated to aiding the understanding of the Border Collie and its breeding. Thanks to this kind of dedication, and to those conscientious handlers and breeders who provide us with first class dogs, the Border Collie's future as a perfect working partner is assured; thanks are also due to the International Sheep Dog Society that has done so much to encourage careful and selective breeding.

At the End of the Day

There is no time limit on training a dog to work: some are slower to develop than others, and some take longer to comprehend the basics of training. It is unwise to make a decision on a collie's capabilities under the age of two years, for many a youngster which appeared to show no potential at one year old has matured and gone on to be a good working dog. Similarly a six-months old collie full of potential and keen to work can be pushed and schooled to the point of sheer boredom. You are not in a race, and the important thing for you to remember is that you are training your own dog to do what you want. It really doesn't matter if your best friend's dog is gathering sheep from the moors and competing on the trials field at 12 months; yours does not have to follow the same pattern, nor do you know how well your friend's dog will be working when it is six years old! Throughout your dog's training, and indeed for the whole of his working life, remember the following tenets:

• Whether you are training your dog to work sheep or cattle, and be it for trialling, for working on the farm or both, you must work at a pace which suits both you and your dog. It is a mistake to think that once you have taught the basics to your dog that training is almost complete, just as it is a mistake to think that learning for your dog is over as soon as he is able to do a reasonable job of work for you. The saying 'you can't teach an old dog new tricks' may hold some truth, but just as we continue to learn as we mature, so will your collie continue to improve.
• From the moment a puppy leaves the security of the nest, its mind is ready to pick up any information you wish to feed to it, and Border Collies in particular are greedy for information. It is therefore important that you provide what you wish your youngster to learn, and that you present it in a way it finds easy to understand.
• Try to make a conscious effort not to be too rigid with your training. No other person will

---

know your dog quite like you, and there is no rule that says you must train him every day, or that each training session must last exactly ten minutes. Each dog is different, and some need all of ten minutes just to settle down, whereas others are losing concentration after only five.

• Always be receptive to your dog's needs: if it appears he is becoming stale, or even too keen, you will do less harm by keeping him away from sheep for a while, than by putting (unnecessary) pressure on him.

• Whilst training your dog we have explained how to restrict his options, such that when you want him to walk behind you don't allow him in front, and when you ask him to come back to you, you make sure that a light line prevents him from doing otherwise. Similarly, you should restrict your own options to prevent making mistakes: thus, if you are not in the mood for training, or feel short of patience, take him for a walk instead, because it is foolish to take a young dog to sheep if you are not ready to enjoy it.

• Feed your dog a sensible diet to ensure that he is fit enough, but not so fit that he finds it hard to listen to you because he has so much pent-up energy.

• Leave your stick behind until you have taught your dog the basics because a sensitive youngster can soon become stick-shy, and often without realizing the effect you have had on his sensibilities until it is too late.

• If you acquire your dog as a puppy, make sure that both you and he enjoy his puppyhood because it is all too short a time, and it is one of the best periods for bonding. There must be very few people who can resist the appeal of a puppy, and it is a very special feeling to have a pair of trusting little blue eyes watching and waiting for you. Try to make sure that, no matter how busy you are, you spend some quality time with your youngster each day, not just training and learning but a companionable time when you can enjoy each other's company. The more time you spend with your pup, the more you will have to look

Spot makes sure that the dairy cows do not take the wrong turning on their way to the pasture down the lane.

A road full of sheep. Mrs Curwen and Tom Dickinson take the hill flock of Swaledale ewes back to the homestead after a four-hour gather off the fells.

back on, and when your training seems to be at a standstill you will be able to look back on the little chap who didn't even know his name when you first met him, and then you will realize just how much you have both learnt.

• The young Border Collie may be impetuous and eager to please, so it is your responsibility to keep the training to a sensible pace; learning to understand his moods and his body language, because he will certainly be able to understand yours.

• Try to relax when you are training: tension only creates tension, and you are not only training, but trying to fashion an important partnership. Thus, when you take your dog to the field take some deep breaths, get rid of any nerves you may be harbouring, and instead of creating problems or mentally fighting your dog, just relax and enjoy every second spent training him. It is both a creative and pleasurable time, and the end result, a working partnership, is something to be proud of.

• The term 'man's best friend' has described the dog for centuries, and various breeds past and present have served mankind in different ways, as guard, companion, hunter and sled dog. Some breeds have merged into one, either by necessity or even because of threat of extinction, but they have all earned their place in history. The Border Collie, however, far from facing extinction as have some of the other herding dogs, has gone from strength to strength, developing an empathy with mankind and thus making it possible to form a valuable working partnership with him. Throughout the formative years of your dog's life, and in all his training it is this empathy for which you are striving, because without it you may never be able to appreciate that special feeling of a dog giving you one hundred per cent of unquestioned devotion.

• A Border Collie does not find it difficult to be faithful, and will sometimes stick by you even when it is not deserved; but training alone does not guarantee the devotion of your dog – this has to be earned. Then you will have one of the most loyal partners you could ever wish for.

• Do not underestimate your dog's mental capacity. You are training him in the hope that, whether he is working a lowland field or on the hills, he will be able to judge how best to handle the stock and any situation which may arise, even when you are out of both sight and earshot. He does not switch his brain off when he is not working, he still has the ability to work things out, and although you may not always appreciate it, he will sense your moods and will react accordingly.

• A trained Border Collie is willing to work with you, be it as sheep dog, guard dog, companion, or whatever lifestyle you choose, so it is worth taking time not only to train your dog, but to get to know him.

• Once your dog has matured and is able to do the work required of him, you still need to take time to understand his needs: if your work allows you to have your dog with you throughout the day, take him too so you can continue to build on your relationship; but don't make the end of your working day the end of your dog's day. Just as you need some form of relaxation, so does your partner, so make sure you either share a walk together or he has some free time rolling, playing and enjoying himself before he goes to his kennel for the night. And if you are limited as to the amount of time you can have your dog with you during the day, then all the more reason for you to make sure you have some quality time together when you return home from work.

Because at the end of the day you will not only have a valuable working partner to be proud of, but you will be able to enjoy the company of your own intelligent, thinking Border Collie.

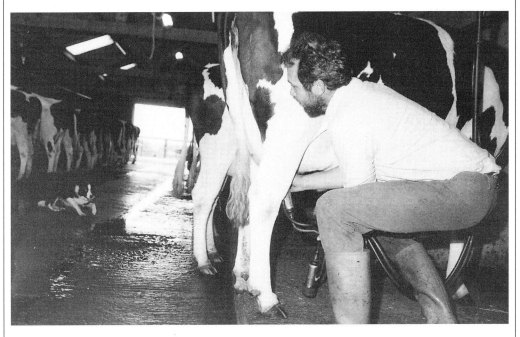

Spot waits patiently as the last cow is milked before taking them back to the field to graze.

141

Glossary

away to me	right-hand command.
basics	foundation training.
BVA	British Veterinary Association.
cast	dog's natural outrun.
CEA	collie eye anomaly.
CHD	canine hip dysplasia.
clock theory	used to describe the dog and handler's position round the sheep.
come by	left-hand command.
complete food	prepacked dried food, an all-in-one mixture.
dam	mother.
drive	driving the sheep away from the handler.
ewe	female sheep.
eye	the power in the collie's eye to hold or move stock.
fetch	term used to describe the act of bringing the sheep to the fold.
freeze	the dog hypnotized by the sheep.
give voice	to bark.
heavy sheep	slow-moving sheep.
holding	the dog keeping the sheep still in one place.
ISDS	International Sheep Dog Society.
lift	the first contact the dog makes with the sheep to move them to the handler.
look back	to send the dog back for more sheep.
natural balance	the dog's natural ability to hold the sheep to the handler.
nursery trial	trial for beginner dogs.
outrun	the line the dog takes to go round the sheep.
PRA	progressive retinal atrophy.
progeny	offspring.
ram	male sheep.
shed	separating two or more sheep from the flock.
single	separating one sheep from the flock.
sire	father.
six o'clock	the handler's position to the dog.
stalker	dog slinking low on the ground.
take time	term used to slow the dog down.
that'll do	recall command.
twelve o'clock	the dog round the sheep opposite the handler.
weakness	the dog's inability to move sheep masterfully.

Index